SO, WHAT CAN I EAT NOW?!

LIVING WITHOUT DAIRY, SOY, EGGS, AND WHEAT

HEALTHY AND DELICIOUS RECIPES WITHOUT COMPROMISING FLAVOR—LOW FAT • LOW CALORIES • LOW SUGAR • LOW SODIUM

Rhonda Peters

Book Division of Rhonda's Cooking, LLC

Published by Rhonda's Cooking, LLC
5130 West Baseline Road
Suite 117, PMB 118
Laveen, Arizona 85339

Chief Creative Director: Clemille Peters, Jr.
Interior Layout and Design: Clemille Peters, Jr. and Krause Creative
Cover Design: Krause Creative
Photography: Chris Marchetti Photography
Food Stylists: Emily Bolton and Rhonda Peters
Assistant Food Stylists: Chris Marchetti and Dave Branstrator
Copyediting: Glory Davis, Susan Coartney, and Lubertha Peters

Peters, Rhonda.
So, What Can I Eat Now?!

Library of Congress Control Number: 2009924889

ISBN-13: 978-0-615-28593-1

Distributed by Emerald Book Company

For ordering information or special discounts for bulk purchases, please contact Emerald Book Company at PO Box 91869, Austin, TX 78709, 512.891.6100.

Part of the Tree Neutral® program, which offsets the number of trees consumed in the production and printing of this book by taking proactive steps, such as planting trees in direct proportion to the number of trees used: www.treeneutral.com

TreeNeutral

Developed and Designed in the United States of America
Printed in Thailand

Contents

Acknowledgements

There were so many friends, family members, and acquaintances that supported and encouraged me in a variety of ways as I wrote So What Can I Eat Now. I would like to take this opportunity to thank each of them.

The highest praise and thanks go to God for giving me the inspiration and endurance to write this book. I am grateful that He has given me an opportunity and a platform to share my experiences and to inspire people with various health challenges to eat a nutritious, life-supporting diet.

Sincere thanks to my wonderful mother and friend, Lubertha Peters, an awesome cook whom I credit for teaching me the fundamentals and techniques of cooking. When I struggled with the last phase of writing this project, my mom was a very encouraging recipe editor and tester who motivated me whenever I felt like quitting. Thanks also to my dad, Clemille Peters, Sr. for supporting and encouraging me daily, for showing interest in the cookbook and for promoting it to his co-workers and acquaintances. I value my parent's devotion and want them to know that it was indeed a blessing to finish writing my book in the home where I first learned to cook—at home in Angie, Louisiana.

Words cannot express my gratefulness to my brother, Clemille Peters, Jr., for his major contribution as chief creative director and graphic designer. From the front cover to the back, he has done a phenomenal job. As coach, encourager, and supporter throughout this journey, he was always there to listen to me as I brainstormed even though he was busy with launching Konsole Kingz, LLC. Thanks to my sister-in-law, Antoinette Peters, for allowing me to retreat at their home for 9 days as I worked on this book.

Heartfelt appreciation goes to Pastor Moore and Minister Erica Moore for being my first recipe testers. Special appreciation to Minister Erica for being open-minded and willing to test my concept recipes. I am also thankful for her clever and constructive feedback.

Thanks to Mrs. Emily Bolton for being my sous-chef and food stylist during the photo shoot. I could not have survived without her that day! Thanks to Chris Marchetti and Dave of Marchetti Photography for being compassionate and willing to help even if it meant being a food stylist! I am also appreciative to Carrie Hernandez for taking care of me at the end of the photo shoot.

Sincere thanks to Kurt Krause of Krause Creative. Kurt's commitment, professionalism and design experience were instrumental to this book. He stepped in and delivered an impressive cover design and brought closure to this project.

Thanks to the best nationally certified English teacher of all-time, Glory Davis, my former high school English teacher. At the last minute, Ms. Davis rearranged her schedule to assist me with editing parts of this book. Thanks for always being available.

Finally, I acknowledge the following people who, in one way or the other, were instrumental in making this book a success: Dr. Victor and Catherine Eagan, Kimberly Dellafosse, Patricia Fuller, Geri Gonzales, Shavon Griffin, Monique Hayward, Kesha Hodge, Pastor Sidney Jones and Mrs. Jones, Tammye Keegan, Paulette Laster, Dr. Leon, Justine Lopez, Leah Martin, Stephanie Monarch, Christian Mordh, Elaine Cauley, Sherry Moss, Emma Ross, Nefertari Thomas, Daniel and Kendra Tillman, and Wealthy Women Club Members.

Foreword

There are many books available to the public in the fields of nutrition and alternative medicine. It is difficult for the public to sift through the varying opinions of how we should eat. As a Naturopathic Physician of 16 years I have seen how difficult it can be for patients to know how to eat. Or they have great knowledge of balanced eating but are frustrated by their lack of sufficient results.

In this thought then, it is often a personal experience which makes the greatest impact upon us. In presenting this nutritional information, Rhonda not only utilizes her years of cooking experience but brings into her work the disciplines of methodical scientific analysis.

I have seen in her as well as with many patients the impact of foods on health and in the function or dysfunction of the body. Many do not realize that the foods which they are consuming are adding to their health complaints. Naturopathic Medicine takes the position that indeed we are what we eat and seeks to identify in every individual their unique nutritional requirements.

A strong example of this is the fact that while the grains provide nutrients and fulfillment in the dining experience, some cannot tolerate the gluten components within them. And so what would normally be a healthy and reasonable recommendation for one may not work for another.

The world of cooking and nutrition are wrought with traditions sometimes not based on true understandings of the science of the human body. Rhonda offers her unbiased perspective on the challenges of educating the public about their food options.

Her knowledge of mathematics and physics and their application to food preparation makes this book not only unique but also extremely helpful.

Rhonda's work will no doubt be a great service to humanity furthering our knowledge of nutrition and cooking.

Therefore I am profoundly pleased and honored to recommend her book to anyone who would be bold enough to "go outside the box" in exploring their eating options.

Dr. Gilberto Leon NMD

About the Author

Rhonda is a Diet Counselor and Certified Professional Food Manager with over 10 years of engineering and business experience in the high-technology industry. She has coached a number of clients and taught them about healthier food alternatives in order to help them feel great physically and mentally. Since learning about her intolerance to dairy, soy and eggs, Rhonda has been on a quest to convert the traditional southern meals that she grew up eating in Louisiana to accommodate her new diet.

Through extensive research and testing, Rhonda has developed a number of healthy breakfast foods, appetizers, entrees and desserts that can offer people alternative, delicious meals that are healthy with excellent flavors.

Rhonda is a member of The Food Allergy and Anaphylaxis Network (FAAN), Celiac Disease Foundation, American Heart Association, and American Diabetes Association. Rhonda is also the Phoenix Gluten-free Food Examiner for Examiner.com.

Introduction

I grew up in a small town called Angie, which is about 100 miles north of New Orleans, Louisiana. With a population of less than 5000, Angie is a place where basically everyone knows everyone. When I was growing up, there was no McDonald's, Boston Market, or Popeye's in my neck of the woods. Consequently, we had home cooked meals everyday; there were no days off in our kitchen! Everyday my mother made certain that we had a good hot breakfast and a full course meal for dinner!

Seafood Gumbo, fried catfish and hush puppies, smothered pork chops with rice and gravy, chicken and dumplings, greens and cornbread cooked with smoked ham hocks, peach cobbler, red velvet cake, and the list goes on. These are just a few of the wonderful dishes that my mother made that were typical of Angie and other Southern towns. Yes, my mother was an excellent cook, and everyone bragged on her chili, gumbo, and pecan pie.

With a mother like that, it was inevitable that I would follow her footsteps. I have been cooking since the age of 9, starting with my award winning, blue ribbon Southern pecan pie. Later I moved to other traditional Southern dishes such as fried chicken, cornbread dressing, red beans & rice, and collard greens. By age 12, I had learned to cut a whole chicken into its eight main parts. And I had mastered the art of momma's secret seasoning.

When I graduated from college and moved into my own apartment, I really put my skills to use. I cooked daily. I loved getting into the kitchen to create—it was therapeutic! It was so exciting to taste the food and give it the "just like mom's" stamp of approval. As years passed, I gained knowledge about other types of cuisines such as Italian and Chinese and later learned to cook some of those recipes. Even though these recipes where good, I would still infuse my Louisiana spices into each dish. For, I enjoyed eating these rich, spicy, salty and sugary foods typical of my area.

THE CHANGE...

When I was twenty-three years old, my health changed drastically. I had problems with my thyroid gland and joints in my hands. After seeing a number of doctors and specialists, I learned that I had hyperthyroidism and rheumatoid arthritis. I was in shock! Then, I knew nothing of a thyroid, and as for arthritis, I thought that was an old folk's disease. After all, that's what my grandma had. So, what did all of this mean for me? Well, for years it meant a physical and emotional, "yo-yo" lifestyle where things would go from one extreme to the next in a very short time. Because my immune system was dysfunctional, my body literally worked against me. My weight fluctuated and my vision weakened. My hands swelled so much that I could not grip a toothbrush, zip my clothes, or drive.

I tried many new drugs to help me feel better. For the hyperthyroidism, I took various doses of synthyroid, as well as the radioactive iodine treatment. The radioactive iodine cured the hyperthyroidism, but over time left me with hypothyroidism. For the treatment for the arthritis, let's just say that whenever the FDA approved a new drug for arthritis, my doctor introduced it to me and I was sure to test it out. Two of the many drugs that I used to help me relieve the pain of the rheumatoid arthritis were VIOXX® and Celebrex. Unfortunately, neither of these helped me on a long term basis. Overtime I accepted the fact that I would have "flare-ups" of inflammation in my wrists twice a year from arthritis. In a like manner, I expected the excessive weight gain due to thyroid imbalance. After seven years of pain and frustration, I met Dr. Don Colbert, Director of The Divine Health Wellness Center, who introduced me to naturopathic medicine. He expressed the importance of living a healthy life by making a few adjustments to reduce stress and to eat healthier. I purchased two of Dr. Colbert's books, one on arthritis and the other on thyroid disease. After reading those two books, I learned many new things about autoimmune diseases. At that point, I decided to consult with a naturopathic physician.

THE REVELATION

Based on a saliva test administered by my naturopathic doctor, I learned that I had intolerances to dairy (specifically to the casein, a milk protein), soy and eggs. I was in shock and heartbroken because I knew that I could no longer eat the down-home southern foods that I loved so well. My first thoughts were how I am going to bake cakes and pies? What about my café latte and cappuccino? After learning about my intolerances, I decided to begin a new journey in life, one that would take me far away from my days as a little girl in Angie, Louisiana, one that would free me from the pain and frustration of my thyroid and arthritis diseases—a life free of dairy, soy and eggs.

WHERE DO I GO FROM HERE?

After thirty-two years of Louisiana soul food, where do I go from here? Considering the fact that I have a Bachelor's Degree in Physics and a Master's in Electrical Engineering, I had lots of experience in solving problems through research, so I embraced my new challenge scientifically. My first step was to start with the basics. I went back to all of my recipes, especially my favorites and then began to study the purpose of each ingredient in them. I prioritized the importance of each of my favorite dishes and then started the study with desserts, which happens to be one of my most favorite things to eat. I had no idea how I would re-create the desserts I grew up eating and make them taste good without dairy and egg.

I sought the answer in cookbooks that I collected over the years. The biggest thing that stood out the most was that majority of them did not accommodate my new diet. So, I found myself researching magazines, health journals and the Internet to see how I could cook without dairy, soy or eggs. The more I researched, the more I learned that there have been many books and studies published that analyzes the direct impact of dairy, soy and eggs on rheumatoid arthritis and thyroid disease, as well as other diseases. However, none of these cookbooks had recipes that addressed all three of my intolerances simultaneously. Frustrated, disgusted I threw up my hands and screamed, "So, What Can I Eat Now?!" I knew that I had to create my own book.

THE PURPOSE OF THIS BOOK

My purpose is to give people challenged with weight fluctuations, food allergies/intolerances, autoimmune diseases, and heart diseases hope. I want them to know that they are not alone, that they can enjoy food even if they are burdened with these potentially life threatening illnesses! Specifically, the purpose of this book is as follows:

1. To develop recipes that are 100% free of the three most common allergens, dairy, soy and eggs.
2. To provide recipes that are low in sodium, sugar, fat, and calories that are an excellent diet for people with diabetes, high cholesterol and high blood pressure.
3. To devise healthy and tasteful recipes that minimize complications with diseases such as arthritis and hypo/hyperthyroidism.
4. To create gluten-free recipes for people who are gluten intolerant.
5. Lastly, to empower and teach all people how to cook healthy foods that taste delicious.

Decoding the Nutrition Facts

The nutrition facts for each recipe in this cookbook were calculated based on an average daily 2000 calorie American diet using the Food Processor SQL Software by Esha Research, Inc. Readers are advised to consult a health care provider before making any dietary changes.

CALORIES
Calories are units of energy and refer to the amount of energy in food and the amount of energy the body uses. Carbohydrates, fats and proteins are sources of calories found in food, whereas vitamins, minerals, cholesterol and fiber do not. In this example, 2000 calories are required, and this recipe only makes up 257 calories of the total amount required.

CHOLESTEROL
Cholesterol is a substance found in foods of animal origin and in every body cell. It is recommended that a person in good health consume no more than 300mg of cholesterol per day. However, if a person is at risk of heart disease, then he/she should consume less than 200mg of cholesterol daily.

SODIUM
Sodium is one of the major trace minerals with important properties in its natural state that the body utilizes. This example recipe only has 480mg of sodium, which is less than the 2400mg daily recommended value. However, consume less than 1800mg of sodium daily if diagnosed with hypertension. (Note: 1 teaspoon salt = 2400mg sodium!)

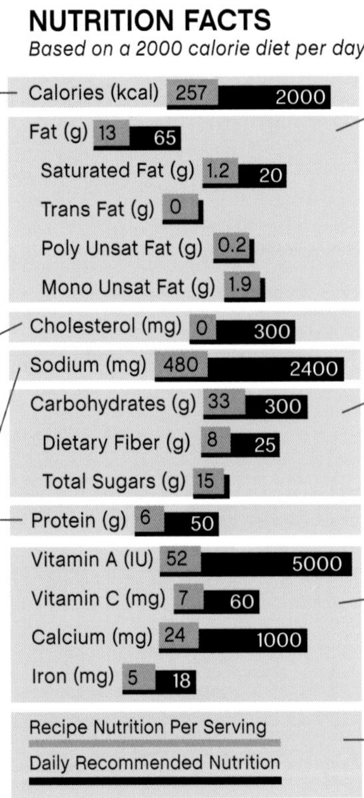

FAT
Fats supply energy and many body processes. They consist of both saturated and unsaturated fats. Strive for low saturated fats and little to none trans fat (<0.1); select foods high in unsaturated fats. The total amount of fat recommended in this example is 65g, and the recipe has only 13g of fat.

CARBOHYDRATES (ALSO KNOWN AS CARBS)
Carbohydrates are made up of sugars, starches, and fibers. Sugar and starches are the body's main source of energy. Consumption amount depends on one's total calorie need; in this example, based on a 2000 calorie diet, 300g of carbohydrates are recommended, but this recipe only contains 33g.

VITAMINS AND MINERALS
Vitamins and minerals regulate several processes in the body that produce energy and more. In fact, they are important in every process that occurs in the body! This label shows that 5000IUs of Vitamin A are recommended based upon a 2000 calorie diet, but this recipe only contains 52IUs.

NUTRITION FACTS (PER SERVING)
The nutrition facts label indicates the total amount of nutrition per serving for this recipe (gray boxes) in comparison to the standard daily 2000 calorie diet for an adult in the USA (black boxes).

PROTEIN
Proteins build, repair and maintain all of the body tissues. They are the body's other source of energy, when carbohydrates are in short supply. Consumption amount depends on one's body weight; in this example, based on a 2000 calorie diet, 50g of protein are recommended, but this recipe only contains 6g.

BREAKFAST

Pancake Sandwich

Total Servings: 3
Serving Size: 1 sandwich

This recipe was created because I didn't have time to sit down to eat pancakes with syrup. I thought about all of the breakfast sandwiches that I used to eat on the go, and decided to make a breakfast pancake sandwich! Pancake sandwiches are fun to make for both kids and adults especially when using various shapes; it definitely brought out the kid in me!

4 tablespoons ground flaxseeds

⅔ cup plus 6 tablespoons water

1½ cups gluten-free all-purpose flour (or whole wheat flour)

1 teaspoon baking powder

½ teaspoon baking soda

⅛ teaspoon Celtic Sea Salt® Brand

¼ teaspoon ground cinnamon

1 tablespoon agave nectar syrup (or ⅛ teaspoon powder Stevia)

½ teaspoon vanilla extract

1½ tablespoons olive oil (or grapeseed oil)

2 tablespoons unsalted almond butter (or pecan butter)

3 small (6-inch) ripe bananas, thinly sliced (or 3 tablespoons fruit spread)

1. Heat a large non-stick skillet over medium heat for 8 to 10 minutes. Whisk 2 tablespoons of the ground flaxseeds and 6 tablespoons of the water in a small bowl with a wire whisk; let stand for 2 to 3 minutes. The consistency should be similar to an egg that has been beaten.
2. Mix flour, baking powder, baking soda, salt, cinnamon, agave syrup, vanilla extract, ½ tablespoon of the olive oil and the remaining ⅔ cup water in a large bowl by hand. Stir in, slowly, the flaxseed mixture until the batter is smooth, without lumps.
3. Coat the preheated skillet evenly with the remaining 1 tablespoon olive oil; make sure that the oil is evenly distributed. Place pancake molds onto the skillet. Pour ⅛ cup of the pancake batter into the molds and cook over low heat 2 to 3 minutes. You will start to see tiny bubbles in the batter; once the bubbles pop, flip the pancakes with a spatula and cook about 1 minute or less. When done, put pancakes into a container and cover. Repeat this step until all batter has been cooked.
4. Mix the remaining 2 tablespoons ground flaxseeds and almond butter with a large spoon until well mixed.
5. Spread 1 teaspoon of the almond butter mixture onto one side of each pancake. Put two banana slices onto the almond butter side of one of the pancakes. Top with the second pancake (almond butter side down). Continue assembling until all sandwiches have been made.

NUTRITION FACTS

Based on a 2000 calorie diet per day

	Recipe Nutrition Per Serving	Daily Recommended Nutrition
Calories (kcal)	257	2000
Fat (g)	13	65
Saturated Fat (g)	1.2	20
Trans Fat (g)	0	
Poly Unsat Fat (g)	0.2	
Mono Unsat Fat (g)	1.9	
Cholesterol (mg)	0	300
Sodium (mg)	480	2400
Carbohydrates (g)	33	300
Dietary Fiber (g)	8	25
Total Sugars (g)	15	
Protein (g)	6	50
Vitamin A (IU)	52	5000
Vitamin C (mg)	7	60
Calcium (mg)	24	1000
Iron (mg)	5	18

Creamy Buckwheat Cereal

Total Servings: 1
Serving Size: 1 cup

I grew up eating grits topped with butter and salt almost every morning for breakfast! However, when I was forced to find new breakfast foods that were gluten-free and corn-free, I found a whole grain cereal called buckwheat. I was definitely surprised to see that the texture of cooked buckwheat looked similar to grits, but cooked in less than 15 minutes! Though the flavor is not the same as grits, buckwheat cereal is a close substitute for me!

¼ cup creamy buckwheat cereal

1 cup water

⅛ teaspoon Celtic Sea Salt® Brand

¼ teaspoon cinnamon

1 tablespoon chopped walnuts

2 tablespoons raisins (or currants)

Add buckwheat cereal, water and salt to a small saucepan and bring to a boil. Stir often and cook, covered, over medium heat, approximately 10 to 15 minutes. If desired, add an additional 1 tablespoon water if buckwheat is too thick; continue adding water until desired consistency. Garnish with cinnamon, walnuts and raisins.

Tidbits

For extra Omega 3 fatty acid, add 1 tablespoon flaxseed oil before eating—do not add during the cooking process as this will destroy the nutrients and possibly make the oil rancid.

Substitute the buckwheat with old-fashioned rolled oats if you are not gluten intolerant. Add 1 teaspoon honey during cooking process when oats are used.

NUTRITION FACTS

Based on a 2000 calorie diet per day

	Recipe Nutrition Per Serving	Daily Recommended Nutrition
Calories (kcal)	320	2000
Fat (g)	5	65
Saturated Fat (g)	0.4	20
Trans Fat (g)	0	
Poly Unsat Fat (g)	1.5	
Mono Unsat Fat (g)	2.8	
Cholesterol (mg)	0	300
Sodium (mg)	207	2400
Carbohydrates (g)	57	300
Dietary Fiber (g)	8	25
Total Sugars (g)	12	
Protein (g)	7	50
Vitamin A (IU)	19	5000
Vitamin C (mg)	1	60
Calcium (mg)	107	1000
Iron (mg)	4	18

Recipe Nutrition Per Serving

Daily Recommended Nutrition

French Toast

Total Servings: 2
Serving Size: 2 slices of bread

Yes, this is correct—French toast can be made without eggs, dairy, or soy! This awesome recipe is a great new twist on the classic French toast recipe without compromising the flavor.

1 tablespoon olive oil

1 tablespoon ground flaxseeds

3 tablespoons water

¼ cup rice milk

1 teaspoon ground cinnamon

1 teaspoon agave nectar syrup (or ⅛ teaspoon Stevia extract)

4 slices brown rice bread (or stone ground whole wheat bread)

1 Heat olive oil in a large non-stick skillet over medium heat for 8 to 10 minutes. Whisk ground flaxseeds and water in a small bowl with a large wire whisk; let stand about 2 to 3 minutes. The consistency should be similar to an egg that has been beaten.

2 Whisk the flaxseed mixture, milk, cinnamon, and syrup in an 8 x 8-inch square pan.

3 Soak one slice of the bread in the liquid mixture until just saturated, about 15 seconds per side. Transfer to a wire rack and repeat with the remaining 3 bread slices. Put soaked bread slices onto the pre-heated skillet and cook over medium-high heat about 3 to 5 minutes. Flip with a spatula and cook on the other side 3 to 5 minutes, or until no longer soft in the middle. (If desired, serve with 1 tablespoon agave nectar syrup or Grade A medium Amber maple syrup.)

Tidbit

Do not allow the bread to soak in the batter because it will be over saturated (soggy) in the middle.

NUTRITION FACTS

Based on a 2000 calorie diet per day

	Recipe Nutrition Per Serving	Daily Recommended Nutrition
Calories (kcal)	327	2000
Fat (g)	18	65
Saturated Fat (g)	1.2	20
Trans Fat (g)	0	
Poly Unsat Fat (g)	0.5	
Mono Unsat Fat (g)	6	
Cholesterol (mg)	0	300
Sodium (mg)	209	2400
Carbohydrates (g)	39	300
Dietary Fiber (g)	4	25
Total Sugars (g)	4	
Protein (g)	4	50
Vitamin A (IU)	74	5000
Vitamin C (mg)	0.2	60
Calcium (mg)	78	1000
Iron (mg)	2	18

Recipe Nutrition Per Serving

Daily Recommended Nutrition

Nut Butter Delight

Total Servings: 1
Serving Size: 1 tablespoon

I absolutely love nuts and I eat them in any way you can imagine—raw, roasted, sweetened, and salted. I even love to eat them when they are ground into a delicious nut butter spread. This recipe is very simple and requires very minimal work.

1 tablespoon ground flaxseeds

1 tablespoon unsalted almond butter

Mix ground flaxseeds and almond butter in a small bowl with a large spoon. If desired, serve on top of rice cakes or toast, or use as a veggie or fruit dip.

Tidbits

There are other nut butters available, just choose your favorite or you can make your own. If you like pecans, try this recipe: Spread 1 pound pecans (shelled and halved) on an ungreased baking sheet. Bake in a pre-heated 350°F oven 8 to 10 minutes. Let toasted nuts cool about 5 minutes. Place toasted pecans into a food processor and process until smooth, about 3 to 5 minutes.

If you are allergic to nuts, substitute the almond butter with 1 ½ tablespoons agave nectar syrup. This syrup mixture is tasty when spread on top of toasted bread or in pancake sandwiches (see pancake sandwich recipe).

NUTRITION FACTS

Based on a 2000 calorie diet per day

	Recipe Nutrition Per Serving	Daily Recommended Nutrition
Calories (kcal)	152	2000
Fat (g)	13	65
Saturated Fat (g)	1.2	20
Trans Fat (g)	0	
Poly Unsat Fat (g)	2	
Mono Unsat Fat (g)	6	
Cholesterol (mg)	0	300
Sodium (mg)	74	2400
Carbohydrates (g)	7	300
Dietary Fiber (g)	4	25
Total Sugars (g)	1	
Protein (g)	4	50
Vitamin A (IU)	0.2	5000
Vitamin C (mg)	0.1	60
Calcium (mg)	44	1000
Iron (mg)	4	18

Recipe Nutrition Per Serving

Daily Recommended Nutrition

APPETIZERS & SNACKS

Twisted Hummus

Total Servings: 6
Serving Size: 2 ounces

After making hummus from a recipe that I found, I was disappointed. So, I set out on a cooking adventure and started creating my version of what I thought hummus should taste like! This recipe is definitely not the traditional hummus flavor; instead, it is my twist on the old. The proportions of salty, sweet and sour make this recipe scrumptious. Many hummus lovers are surprised by the flavors of this recipe when they first taste it; though it's different—they don't stop eating it until it's gone!

1 (15 ounce) can chickpeas or garbanzo beans, rinsed and drained

¼ cup fresh lemon juice

1½ tablespoons tahini

3 tablespoons extra-virgin olive oil

1½ teaspoons ground cumin

1 large clove garlic, minced

2 teaspoons agave nectar syrup

¼ teaspoon Celtic Sea Salt® Brand

⅛ cup water

Put all ingredients into a food processor and process until smooth, approximately 3 to 5 minutes. The hummus should be a soft and creamy consistency similar to that of sandwich spread or mayonnaise. If hummus is still stiff, add 1 or 2 tablespoons water.

Tidbits

To create the traditional hummus flavor, omit the syrup and add an extra 1 tablespoon of lemon juice and an extra 1 large garlic clove.

Hummus can be made with a variety of herbs and vegetables; try adding ½ cup chopped cilantro or ½ cup roasted red bell pepper for a different flavor.

NUTRITION FACTS

Based on a 2000 calorie diet per day

	Recipe Nutrition Per Serving	Daily Recommended Nutrition
Calories (kcal)	132	2000
Fat (g)	9	65
Saturated Fat (g)	1.1	20
Trans Fat (g)	0	
Poly Unsat Fat (g)	2	
Mono Unsat Fat (g)	6	
Cholesterol (mg)	0	300
Sodium (mg)	126	2400
Carbohydrates (g)	12	300
Dietary Fiber (g)	3	25
Total Sugars (g)	3	
Protein (g)	4	50
Vitamin A (IU)	6	5000
Vitamin C (mg)	5	60
Calcium (mg)	28	1000
Iron (mg)	1	18

Recipe Nutrition Per Serving

Daily Recommended Nutrition

Stuffed Mushrooms

Total Servings: 6
Serving Size: 1 stuffed mushroom cap

This is my Louisiana twist on a classic recipe. In my hometown, a popular appetizer is stuffed bell pepper, which is a green bell pepper stuffed with dirty rice. Since I can't eat bell peppers, I decided to take that same concept and stuff the dirty rice into baby Portobello mushrooms.

1 cup cooked brown rice (see recipe)

½ pound ground turkey

3 tablespoons olive oil

½ cup plus 1 tablespoon chopped onions

1 clove garlic, minced

¼ teaspoon crushed red pepper flakes

½ teaspoon Celtic Sea Salt® Brand

1½ tablepsoons onion powder

¾ teaspoon ground sage

Pinch stevia powder

½ cup chopped green onions

¼ teaspoon garlic powder

1½ teaspoons agave nectar syrup

⅛ teaspoon ground white pepper

2 teaspoons balsamic vinegar

6 baby Portobello mushrooms

1 Prepare the brown rice.

2 Heat a large skillet with 2 tablespoons of the olive oil over medium-high heat for 1 to 2 minutes; add chopped onions and garlic and stir, continually about 2 to 3 minutes. Add ground turkey, red pepper flakes, sea salt, 2 ½ teaspoons of the onion powder, ½ teaspoon of the sage, and stevia, and cook, over medium heat breaking up the meat into small pieces with a large spoon, until no longer pink, about 10 to 15 minutes.

3 Stir in the cooked rice, green onions, the remaining 2 teaspoons onion powder, the remaining ¼ teaspoon ground sage, garlic power, agave nectar syrup, white pepper, and balsamic vinegar to the meat and simmer, covered, over low heat about 3 to 5 minutes.

4 Clean the outer skin of the mushrooms with a damp paper towel. Remove the stems from mushrooms using hands; gently scrap away the gills (the soft portion around the stem) with a small spoon and discard.

5 Preheat the oven to 350°F. Arrange the mushroom caps in a non-stick baking dish and spoon dirty rice mixture into caps. Drizzle the remaining 1 tablespoon olive oil over the top of the stuffed mushroom caps and bake for 15 minutes.

Tidbit

Dirty rice typically has a brownish color and many cooks add some sort of artificial coloring; however, I prefer to use balsamic vinegar instead. If you do not have food allergies use soy sauce instead. To make this appetizer vegetarian, simply just eliminate the ground turkey.

NUTRITION FACTS

Based on a 2000 calorie diet per day

	Recipe Nutrition Per Serving	Daily Recommended Nutrition
Calories (kcal)	184	2000
Fat (g)	10	65
Saturated Fat (g)	1	20
Trans Fat (g)	0	
Poly Unsat Fat (g)	1	
Mono Unsat Fat (g)	7	
Cholesterol (mg)	15	300
Sodium (mg)	165	2400
Carbohydrates (g)	12	300
Dietary Fiber (g)	2	25
Total Sugars (g)	3	
Protein (g)	11	50
Vitamin A (IU)	37	5000
Vitamin C (mg)	2	60
Calcium (mg)	22	1000
Iron (mg)	1	18

Recipe Nutrition Per Serving

Daily Recommended Nutrition

Avocado Spread

Total Servings: 12
Serving Size: 2 tablespoons

I developed this recipe because I could not eat mayonnaise and I needed something to spread onto my wraps for moistness. I bought avocados but I really didn't know what to do with them—I didn't even know how to properly peel them; after all, we didn't eat those in Angie, Louisiana! After I figured it out, I combined it with different ingredients that I already had in my pantry. I was pleasantly surprised with the texture, the taste, and the healthiness of this spread! This spread was the highlight of my wrap; I now have hope!

3½ large ripe avocados, rinsed

6 tablespoons extra-virgin olive oil

2 small cloves garlic, crushed

½ medium lime (about 2-inch round), rinsed and peeled

¼ teaspoon Celtic Sea Salt® Brand

1 tablespoon jalapeño pepper, seeded and minced

⅛ cup fresh cilantro leaves (or basil leaves), chopped

1. Slice the avocado in half; remove the seed and the avocado flesh. Discard the seed. (To remove the flesh, position a large spoon between the avocado flesh and skin and slide the spoon around the whole avocado and spoon out the flesh.)
2. Put all ingredients in a food processor (or high-powered blender) and process, until smooth about 2 to 3 minutes.

Tidbits

Avocados are grown in different regions and may look slightly different. Select avocados that yield slightly to the touch—these typically have skins that are a combination of green and brown colors. If avocados are really soft and mostly brown in color, be careful because it may be rotten on the inside.

This spread can also be served as a dip. Reduce the oil to 3 tablespoons and add ½ cup chopped tomatoes or salsa.

NUTRITION FACTS

Based on a 2000 calorie diet per day

Nutrient	Recipe Nutrition Per Serving	Daily Recommended Nutrition
Calories (kcal)	156	2000
Fat (g)	16	65
Saturated Fat (g)	2.3	20
Trans Fat (g)	0	
Poly Unsat Fat (g)	2	
Mono Unsat Fat (g)	11	
Cholesterol (mg)	0	300
Sodium (mg)	39	2400
Carbohydrates (g)	6	300
Dietary Fiber (g)	4	25
Total Sugars (g)	0.5	
Protein (g)	1	50
Vitamin A (IU)	105	5000
Vitamin C (mg)	7	60
Calcium (mg)	9	1000
Iron (mg)	0.4	18

Pesto

Total Servings: 12
Serving Size: ⅛ cup

After seeing all of the beautiful fresh basil at the farmers market, I decided to make some pesto! There are two words that can be used to describe this sauce—rich and buttery. Pesto is so versatile; it can be used as a dipping sauce with your favorite bread or mixed with your favorite pasta or rice. The natural oils from the pine nuts combined with the olive oil and basil add to the richness of this recipe.

4 medium cloves garlic, crushed

¼ cup pine nuts

¾ cup extra-virgin olive oil

2 ounces fresh basil leaves (about 4½ cups, loosely packed)

½ teaspoon Celtic Sea Salt® Brand

Add basil, garlic, pine nuts, and ¼ cup of the oil to a food processor and process to a rough paste, about 2 to 3 minutes. With the machine running, slowly add the remaining ½ cup oil and process until the leaves have been finely chopped, about 1 minute. You will still see small pieces of pine nuts.

Tidbits

Substitute the pine nuts with about ⅓ cup macadamia nuts to put a different spin on the traditional pesto. Macadamia nuts are sweeter, harder and larger than the pine nuts, so add an additional 1 or 2 tablespoons of extra-virgin olive oil. They are excellent heart and thyroid friendly nuts with higher monounsaturated fat (the good fat) than pine nuts.

When using the pesto as a wet rub or as a stuffing, reduce the amount of oil by half.

NUTRITION FACTS

Based on a 2000 calorie diet per day

	Recipe Nutrition Per Serving	Daily Recommended Nutrition
Calories (kcal)	142	2000
Fat (g)	15	65
Saturated Fat (g)	2	20
Trans Fat (g)	0	
Poly Unsat Fat (g)	2	
Mono Unsat Fat (g)	12	
Cholesterol (mg)	0	300
Sodium (mg)	69	2400
Carbohydrates (g)	1	300
Dietary Fiber (g)	0.2	25
Total Sugars (g)	0.1	
Protein (g)	1	50
Vitamin A (IU)	250	5000
Vitamin C (mg)	1	60
Calcium (mg)	11	1000
Iron (mg)	0.3	18

Red Pepper Spread

Total Servings: 2
Serving Size: ½ cup

Back in the day, I had a recipe for roasted red pepper dip made with cream cheese. Since becoming dairy-free, I decided to see what this dip would taste like without dairy. Needless to say, it's great and versatile. There are many ways to use this spread; whether eating it on your favorite toasted bread or mixing it with your favorite pasta, you will love this spread just the same.

4 large fresh red bell peppers, rinsed

½ tablespoon extra-virgin olive oil

1½ tablespoons balsamic vinegar

¼ teaspoon Celtic Sea Salt® Brand

1 Put oven rack close to the top heating element in the oven. Preheat the oven on high broil. Line the bottom and sides of a large baking sheet with aluminum foil.

2 Place whole peppers on the foil and brush with olive oil. Roast peppers on broil and turn with tongs as needed, until the peppers have blistered or slightly blackened all over. Once blistered, remove the roasted peppers from the oven and put in a gallon size storage bag for 10 to 15 minutes.

3 Cut peppers in half and remove the core and seeds. Scrape off the skins and any remaining seeds with the back of a knife. Combine peeled roasted peppers, balsamic vinegar and salt in a food processor and pulse until the bell peppers have been chopped, about 2 to 3 times. Be careful not to over blend; you want to have some small chunks of bell pepper.

Tidbits

This spread is an excellent base for roasted red pepper salad dressing. Just add more oil until your desired consistency—add in ¼ cup increments.

If you do not have problems with dairy, combine 8 ounces organic cream cheese (softened) with the olive oil, balsamic vinegar, and sea salt in a food processor and process until smooth; then add roasted red bell peppers and pulse 2 or 3 times until well mixed.

NUTRITION FACTS

Based on a 2000 calorie diet per day

	Recipe Nutrition Per Serving	Daily Recommended Nutrition
Calories (kcal)	123	2000
Fat (g)	4	65
Saturated Fat (g)	1	20
Trans Fat (g)	0	
Poly Unsat Fat (g)	0.5	
Mono Unsat Fat (g)	3	
Cholesterol (mg)	0	300
Sodium (mg)	220	2400
Carbohydrates (g)	19	300
Dietary Fiber (g)	6	25
Total Sugars (g)	13	
Protein (g)	3	50
Vitamin A (IU)	9000	5000
Vitamin C (mg)	367	60
Calcium (mg)	20	1000
Iron (mg)	1	18

Trail Mix

Total Servings: 1
Serving Size: ¼ cup

I started making trail mix because many of the ones found in stores were loaded with salt and other items that I could not eat. I wanted a trail mix that was simple and delicious. Wherever I go, I always take my trail mix—I can't leave home without it! If you are looking for an affordable healthy and delightful snack without the unhealthy preservatives, then give this recipe a try!

⅛ cup brown rice puffs (or gluten-free oats)

¼ teaspoon ground cinnamon

1 tablespoon raw pumpkin seeds

1 tablespoon raw sunflower seeds

1 tablespoon raisins (or currants)

½ tablespoon chopped pecans (or any other nuts)

Mix brown rice puffs and cinnamon in a small bowl with a spoon. Stir in the pumpkin seeds, sunflower seeds, raisins, and pecans.

Tidbit

There are many different kinds of dried fruits, nuts, and spices that can be used to make trail mix; use your favorite. Depending on the types of ingredients, this snack is low fat; however, as with anything, you must eat with moderation.

NUTRITION FACTS

Based on a 2000 calorie diet per day

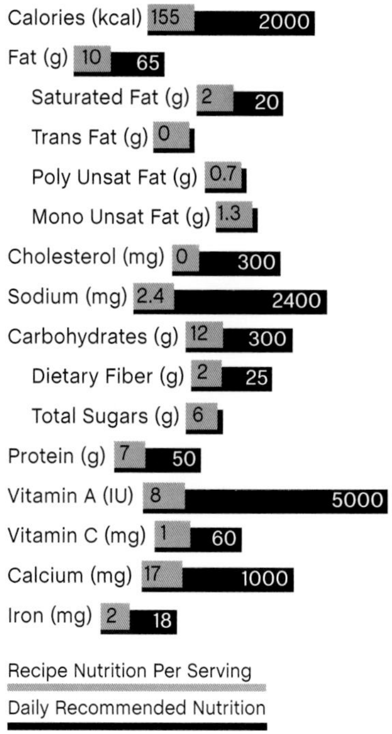

SOUPS, SALADS & SANDWICHES

Chicken Noodle Soup

Total Servings: 6
Serving Size: ¾ cup

A friend of mine was sick and could not eat the traditional canned chicken noodle soup at the local grocery store and her husband turned to me for help. I looked in my pantry and fridge to see what ingredients I had available and immediately went to work. I prepared this savory soup in 30 minutes. It's packed with so much flavor that you would never know that it is gluten-free!

5 skinless chicken breast tenders (about 6 ounces), rinsed

2 cups water

¼ teaspoon Celtic Sea Salt® Brand

5 teaspoons extra-virgin olive oil

1½ cartoons low sodium chicken broth (about 6 cups)

4 ounces dry brown rice fettuccine pasta (or 1 cup cooked brown rice)

½ cup frozen green peas (optional)

1 Add chicken, water, salt and 2 teaspoons of the olive oil to a medium saucepan, and cook, covered, over medium heat about 7 to 8 minutes. Remove chicken breast and dice into small bite-sized cubes; strain stock through a fine mesh strainer into a large bowl and discard any remaining solids. Pour stock back into the pot; add diced chicken and chicken broth. Simmer, covered, over low heat, about 2 to 5 minutes.

2 Fill a large pot three-fourths full of water and add the pasta and the remaining 3 teaspoons olive oil. Stir continuously to prevent the pasta from sticking together and cook, uncovered, over high heat about 7 to 8 minutes. Drain the pasta and rinse under cold water. Add the pasta to the chicken soup; and continue to simmer, covered, stirring often over low heat for 3 to 5 minutes. (If desired, add peas at the same time as cooked pasta.)

Tidbit

Prepare homemade chicken broth by boiling 1 (4-pound) free range whole chicken, 3½ teaspoons salt, 1 medium onion, 3 cloves garlic, 2 sprigs rosemary, 2 sprigs thyme, 6 parsley stalks, ¼ teaspoon black pepper, and 2 teaspoons turmeric in a large pot filled with 8 cups water. Cover and cook over medium heat until done (no pink). If desired, strain using a mesh strainer; save the remaining seasoning and freeze for another soup recipe.

NUTRITION FACTS

Based on a 2000 calorie diet per day

Nutrient	Recipe Nutrition Per Serving	Daily Recommended Nutrition
Calories (kcal)	216	2000
Fat (g)	10	65
Saturated Fat (g)	2	20
Trans Fat (g)	0	
Poly Unsat Fat (g)	1.5	
Mono Unsat Fat (g)	5.6	
Cholesterol (mg)	12	300
Sodium (mg)	273	2400
Carbohydrates (g)	21	300
Dietary Fiber (g)	1	25
Total Sugars (g)	0.4	
Protein (g)	7	50
Vitamin A (IU)	0	5000
Vitamin C (mg)	.02	60
Calcium (mg)	15	1000
Iron (mg)	1	18

Recipe Nutrition Per Serving

Daily Recommended Nutrition

Simple Veggie Soup

Total Servings: 6
Serving Size: 1 cup

My inspiration for creating this soup was weight loss! I wanted a healthy and filling soup during those days I needed to control my calories, carbs and fats! This simple but palatable soup is packed with lots of vitamins and minerals.

- 4 cups water
- 2 cups vegetable broth
- ¾ cup chopped onions
- ½ cup chopped green onions
- 1 tablespoon chopped savory leaves (or ⅛ cup parsley)
- 3 tablespoons chopped cilantro leaves
- ½ cup sliced celery, ¼-inch thick
- 1 cup sliced carrots, ¼-inch thick
- ¾ cup frozen sweet green peas
- ½ cup frozen cut green beans
- ½ teaspoon Celtic Sea Salt® Brand
- ¼ teaspoon garlic powder
- 3 tablespoons onion powder
- Pinch ground cracked black pepper
- ¾ cup cubed white potato

Bring water and vegetable broth to a rolling boil in a 3 quart pot. Add the rest of the ingredients; cover and cook over medium heat about 1 hour. The seasonings will start to come alive after about 30 minutes. If needed, additional salt can be added sparingly in ⅛ teaspoon increments, until desired taste.

Tidbit

Experiment with adding a variety of vegetables, spices and herbs such as stewed tomatoes, asparagus, thyme, etc. Have fun creating your signature version of this soup; you can't go wrong!

NUTRITION FACTS

Based on a 2000 calorie diet per day

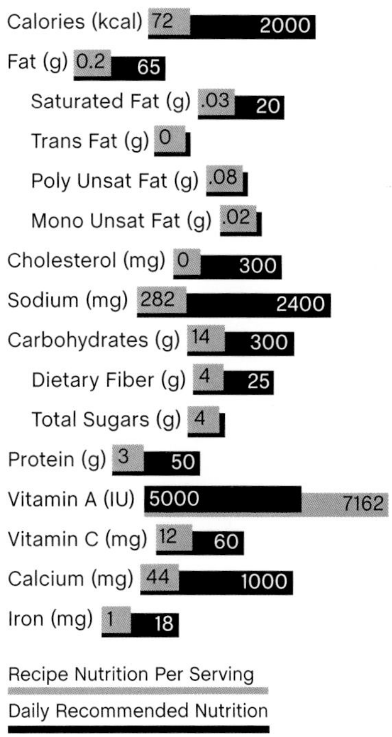

Gumbo

Total Servings: 8
Serving Size: 1 cup

I created this gumbo when I was craving some of my momma's gumbo, which I could no longer eat. Though this gumbo is not the real deal, it is a very close resemblance. This gumbo is a great substitute for people who cannot have shellfish or tomatoes. With the changes that I made with the original recipe, I was so shocked that my new creation was able to capture the essence of Louisiana gumbo. I think you will be pleasantly surprised with the flavor and texture—my mom was!

1½ pounds wild cod fillets, rinsed and cubed (bite-sized)

2 boneless, skinless chicken thighs, rinsed and cubed (optional)

2 quarts water

1 cup chopped green onions

1 cup chopped celery

¾ cup chopped yellow onions

2 tablespoons ground gumbo filé

1½ teaspoons Celtic Sea Salt® Brand

¼ teaspoon granulated garlic

2 tablespoons onion powder

¼ teaspoon red pepper flakes

⅛ teaspoon ground white pepper

2 cups chopped okra

¼ medium fresh beet, without top, rinsed and peeled

1 Add water, green onions, celery and yellow onions to a large pot and bring to a rolling boil. Stir in the gumbo filé, and cook, with the lid semi-covered, over medium heat, until the gumbo filé has dissolved, about 10 to 15 minutes. Add the sea salt, granulated garlic, onion powder, red pepper flakes, white pepper, and okra, stirring often until well mixed; simmer, covered for 15 to 20 minutes, or until the okra is cooked into smaller pieces. (Observe the gumbo mixture periodically to ensure that it does not boil over.)

2 Add the beet to the gumbo for color. (If desired, add cubed chicken during this step.) Reduce heat to medium low and cook, covered, for 3 to 5 minutes (the gumbo mixture will start to change to a maroon color.) Remove the beet once you are satisfied with the color. Stir in the fish and simmer, covered over low heat, until the fish is opaque throughout, about 5 to 8 minutes.

Tidbits

Typically Louisiana gumbo is a brownish red color, and in order to maintain a similar color, I add beet slices to facilitate the color change from green to the brownish-red. Do not leave the beet quarter in the gumbo too long. The longer it is left in the gumbo, the more maroon it will become.

To make the traditional Louisiana gumbo, add the following to this recipe: 1 tablespoon tomato paste (instead of beets), ⅛ teaspoon white pepper, 2 boneless, skinless, chopped chicken thighs, 1 cup diced turkey or chicken sausage, 1 cup deveined shrimp (instead of cod), and 1 cooked dungeon crab broken into pieces; these additions will surely make the gumbo pop!

NUTRITION FACTS

Based on a 2000 calorie diet per day

	Recipe Nutrition Per Serving	Daily Recommended Nutrition
Calories (kcal)	91	2000
Fat (g)	1	65
Saturated Fat (g)	0.1	20
Trans Fat (g)	0	
Poly Unsat Fat (g)	0.3	
Mono Unsat Fat (g)	0.1	
Cholesterol (mg)	31	300
Sodium (mg)	382	2400
Carbohydrates (g)	4	300
Dietary Fiber (g)	2	25
Total Sugars (g)	1	
Protein (g)	16	50
Vitamin A (IU)	198	5000
Vitamin C (mg)	10	60
Calcium (mg)	40	1000
Iron (mg)	1	18

Chili Beans

Total Servings: 4½ cups
Serving Size: 1 cup

I used to love eating chili, but most of the recipes had tomatoes and other ingredients that I could not eat. So naturally, I returned to the kitchen to re-create this old-time classic recipe without tomatoes. This hearty and healthy soup is packed with protein and fiber and it's perfect for those cold days. If you love chili but cannot eat tomatoes, this recipe was modified with you in mind.

1 pound ground chicken breast

1 tablespoon olive oil

½ cup chopped onions

2 large cloves garlic, minced

2 teaspoons red chili pepper flakes

5 teaspoons ground cumin

3 teaspoons chili powder

2 tablespoons onion powder

¾ teaspoon Celtic Sea Salt® Brand

1 teaspoon agave nectar syrup

1¼ cups water

1 (15 ounce can) red beans (about 2 cups), rinsed and drained

1¼ teaspoons fresh beet juice

Heat oil in a large saucepan, over medium heat about 1 to 2 minutes. Add onions and garlic and stir, continually about 1 to 2 minutes. Add ground chicken breast, red chili pepper flakes, cumin, chili powder, onion powder, sea salt, and syrup, breaking up the meat with a large spoon, until no longer pink about 7 to 10 minutes. Stir in the water, red beans, and beet juice and simmer, covered, stirring often, until beans are tender, about 10 to 15 minutes minutes.

Tidbits

If the chili is too thick then add ¼ cup water and ½ teaspoon beet juice; continue adding until desired consistency. Please note that you may need to increase the seasoning if more water is added.

To make traditional chili, use 1 can of stewed tomatoes (or 4 tablespoons of tomato paste) instead of beet juice and 1 teaspoon agave syrup.

NUTRITION FACTS

Based on a 2000 calorie diet per day

	Recipe Nutrition Per Serving	Daily Recommended Nutrition
Calories (kcal)	296	2000
Fat (g)	12	65
Saturated Fat (g)	2.8	20
Trans Fat (g)	0	
Poly Unsat Fat (g)	2.4	
Mono Unsat Fat (g)	5.7	
Cholesterol (mg)	80	300
Sodium (mg)	407	2400
Carbohydrates (g)	20	300
Dietary Fiber (g)	7	25
Total Sugars (g)	2	
Protein (g)	24	50
Vitamin A (IU)	863	5000
Vitamin C (mg)	4	60
Calcium (mg)	99	1000
Iron (mg)	4	18

Rhonda's Greek Salad

Total Servings: 1
Serving Size: 1 salad

I ate my first green salad at the age of twenty-seven! Cold lettuce with all of those raw vegetables never excited me, but thank goodness I have grown up! I have learned to create beautiful, delicious salads using a variety of lettuce, spices, vegetables, and fruit. This particular recipe is one of my favorite salads—it's a twist on the traditional Greek salad. There's not just one way to make a tasty salad. Experiment and have fun with it!

2 cups chopped romaine lettuce

¼ cup cooked chickpeas or garbanzo beans

1½ teaspoons sliced black olives

⅛ cup sliced cucumber, ⅛-inch thick

¼ cup diced cooked beets

¼ cup shredded carrots

¼ cup shredded zuchini

¼ cup sliced red onion, ⅛-inch thick

1 tablespoon grapeseed oil

¼ teaspoon Celtic Sea Salt® Brand (optional)

Arrange romaine lettuce on a large plate. Addchickpeas, olives, cucumber, beets, carrots, zuchini and red onion slices on top of lettuce. Drizzle grapeseed oil over salad. If desired, add salt.

Tidbits

To take this salad to the next level add ¼ cup diced avocado, 1 teaspoon capers, ½ teaspoon crushed red pepper flakes, ½ teaspoon ground Italian seasoning, and ½ teaspoon good aged balsalmic vinegar.

There's just not one way to make a good salad. There are so many varieties of lettuce, herbs and spices, as well as oils and vinegars that can enhance the flavor of a salad. Experiment with different combinations and have fun with it!

NUTRITION FACTS

Based on a 2000 calorie diet per day

	Recipe Nutrition Per Serving	Daily Recommended Nutrition
Calories (kcal)	248	2000
Fat (g)	16	65
Saturated Fat (g)	1.6	20
Trans Fat (g)	0	
Poly Unsat Fat (g)	10	
Mono Unsat Fat (g)	3	
Cholesterol (mg)	0	300
Sodium (mg)	95	2400
Carbohydrates (g)	24	300
Dietary Fiber (g)	8	25
Total Sugars (g)	9	
Protein (g)	7	50
Vitamin A (IU)	13028	5000
Vitamin C (mg)	43	60
Calcium (mg)	85	1000
Iron (mg)	3	18

Not Your Ordinary Taco Salad

Total Servings: 1
Serving Size: 1 salad

I stumbled on brown rice tortillas in the grocery store and decided to experiment with it to revise the traditional taco salad to suit my diet. To my surprise, this salad not only had the look, but also the taste! The combinations of cumin and chili powder, along with the avocado spread, gave this salad the traditional taco salad flavor.

- 3 tablespoons avocado spread (see recipe)
- 1 (8-inch) brown rice flour tortilla (or whole grain flour tortilla)
- 1½ cups chopped romaine lettuce
- 2 tablespoons chopped green onions
- ¼ cup canned black beans, rinsed and drained
- ⅛ cup shredded carrots
- ⅛ teaspoon ground cumin
- ⅛ teaspoon ground chili powder
- ½ tablespoon extra-virgin olive oil (optional)
- ¼ cup cubed tomatoes or salsa (optional)
- ¼ cup cooked ground turkey (optional)

1. Prepare avocado spread.
2. Wrap tortilla between two sheets of paper towels; heat in the microwave for about 15 seconds. Be careful not to over heat.
3. Place the tortilla gently into a 6-inch circular pan and gently and quickly press. Make sure that the tortilla has a flat base like a bowl. Bake in a preheated 400°F oven about 3 to 5 minutes, or until brown. Remove the toasted tortilla, gently, from the pan. It should look like a bowl.
4. Brush 1 tablespoon of the avocado spread, carefully, in the bottom and around the sides of the tortilla shell using a silicone brush or small spoon.
5. Place the lettuce, green onions, black beans, shredded carrots, ground cumin and chili powder in the toasted tortilla shell (in that order). Add remaining 2 tablespoons of avocado spread to the top of the salad. If desired, top salad with olive oil, tomatoes and ground turkey before serving.

Tidbit

Do not eat the shell if you are watching your daily calories and sodium intake. However, if you have a few calories to spare and haven't gone overboard with your total sodium allowance for the day, then eat the shell because it tastes great with the avocado spread!

NUTRITION FACTS

Based on a 2000 calorie diet per day

	Recipe Nutrition Per Serving	Daily Recommended Nutrition
Calories (kcal)	225	2000
Fat (g)	16	65
Saturated Fat (g)	2.3	20
Trans Fat (g)	0	
Poly Unsat Fat (g)	1.7	
Mono Unsat Fat (g)	11	
Cholesterol (mg)	0	300
Sodium (mg)	127	2400
Carbohydrates (g)	19	300
Dietary Fiber (g)	9	25
Total Sugars (g)	4	
Protein (g)	5	50
Vitamin A (IU)	8641	5000
Vitamin C (mg)	25	60
Calcium (mg)	60	1000
Iron (mg)	2	18

Recipe Nutrition Per Serving
Daily Recommended Nutrition

Almost New Orleans Po-boy

Total Servings: 1
Serving Size: 1 sandwich

Leftover pot roast was so exciting in my house because it was an opportunity for us to make those infamous, juicy New Orleans roast beef po-boy sandwiches! Since the main ingredients of a traditional po-boy are French bread, meat, tomatoes and mayonnaise, I had to create my spin on this wonderful New Orleans classic that I grew up eating.

½ cup cooked pot roast (see recipe)

2 tablespoons avocado spread (see recipe)

1 teaspoon olive oil

1 (6-inch) gluten-free bun (or whole grain bread loaf) sliced in half lengthwise

½ small tomato, sliced (about ¼-inch thick)

½ cup shredded iceberg lettuce

1 Prepare pot roast and avocado spread. Break up cooked pot roast into thin shreds by pulling the meat apart with a fork.

2 Heat a medium non-stick skillet (or grill) with ½ teaspoon of the olive oil over medium heat about 2 to 3 minutes; place the bread onto the grill (cut side down) and grill until golden brown, about 3 to 5 minutes.

3 Spread the avocado spread onto the cut sides of each piece of bread. On the bottom piece, add tomato slices, shredded beef and shredded lettuce (layer in that order). Place the other slice of bread on top.

4 Add the remaining ½ teaspoon olive oil to the preheated grill and evenly distribute; place the sandwich in the pan and grill on both sides until golden brown, about 3 to 5 minutes.

Tidbits

For the original New Orleans recipe, add real mayonnaise (instead of avocado spread) and French bread (instead of the gluten-free bun). Be mindful that mayonnaise is made with eggs so do not use if you are allergic to them.

Do NOT be alarmed by the total fat intake in this recipe. The avocado spread contributes 50% of the total fat which is healthy monounsaturated fat—the good fat! Just eat half of the sandwich if fat and carbs are a concern for your diet.

NUTRITION FACTS

Based on a 2000 calorie diet per day

	Recipe Nutrition Per Serving	Daily Recommended Nutrition
Calories (kcal)	568	2000
Fat (g)	27	65
Saturated Fat (g)	4	20
Trans Fat (g)	0	
Poly Unsat Fat (g)	2	
Mono Unsat Fat (g)	13	
Cholesterol (mg)	54	300
Sodium (mg)	613	2400
Carbohydrates (g)	48	300
Dietary Fiber (g)	9	25
Total Sugars (g)	11	
Protein (g)	32	50
Vitamin A (IU)	622	5000
Vitamin C (mg)	15	99
Calcium (mg)	65	1000
Iron (mg)	5	18

Recipe Nutrition Per Serving

Daily Recommended Nutrition

Veggie Sandwich

Total Servings: 1
Serving Size: 1 sandwich

After eating a vegetarian sandwich that I purchased from a local bread bakery, I was so amazed; I never knew that a sandwich could taste so good without meat! So, in an effort to re-create that taste, I created a veggie sandwich that is so good that you will forget about the meat!

2 slices gluten-free bread (or whole grain bread)

2 tablespoons roasted red pepper spread (see recipe)

½ small tomato, sliced round (about ¼-inch thick)

½ fresh zucchini (or cucumber), halved lengthwise (about ¼-inch thick), about 3 or 4 slices

⅛ cup shredded carrots

6 to 9 spinach leaves

1 Prepare roasted red pepper spread.

2 Arrange the 2 slices of bread on a plate and spread roasted red pepper spread on both slices of the bread. Add tomato slices, zucchini slices, shredded carrots, and spinach leaves on one slice of bread and stack the second slice on the top. (If desired, trim zucchini slices to fit neatly on bread.)

Tidbits

To make panini-style, preheat a panini grill machine. Grill zucchini on the panini grill until soft, about 2 to 3 minutes. Assemble sandwich as indicated above in Step 2 and spread the top and bottom with ½ teaspoon olive oil. Grill the sandwich on the grill for 2 to 3 minutes, until golden brown. Cut sandwich in half, and serve warm.

A variety of vegetables and spreads can be used in this recipe. If you cannot have tomatoes and red bell peppers, then substitute with thinly sliced cooked beets and avocado spread (or hummus).

NUTRITION FACTS

Based on a 2000 calorie diet per day

	Recipe Nutrition Per Serving	Daily Recommended Nutrition
Calories (kcal)	226	2000
Fat (g)	1.5	65
Saturated Fat (g)	0.2	20
Trans Fat (g)	0	
Poly Unsat Fat (g)	0.3	
Mono Unsat Fat (g)	0.7	
Cholesterol (mg)	0	300
Sodium (mg)	100	2400
Carbohydrates (g)	32	300
Dietary Fiber (g)	20	25
Total Sugars (g)	7	
Protein (g)	17	50
Vitamin A (IU)	7886	5000
Vitamin C (mg)	123	60
Calcium (mg)	138	1000
Iron (mg)	4	18

Recipe Nutrition Per Serving

Daily Recommended Nutrition

Lady Bug

AB & J Sandwich

Total Servings: 1
Serving Size: 1 sandwich

When I started eating almond butter, I decided to re-create my favorite childhood sandwiches, peanut butter and jelly. Once I tasted this sandwich, I had a flashback moment to lunch time in elementary school!

1 tablespoon unsalted almond butter (or hazelnut butter)

1 tablespoon ground flaxseeds

2 slices gluten-free bread (or any whole grain bread)

1 tablespoon blueberry spread (or other fresh fruits/spreads)

1. Mix almond butter and ground flaxseeds in a small bowl with a fork.
2. Arrange bread on a plate; spread almond butter mixture on one side of both slices of bread; spread blueberry spread on top of the almond butter mixture. Press both slices together.

Tidbits

If the almond butter mixture is stiff and somewhat dry, add an additional 1 or 2 teaspoons almond butter.

Try other nut butters for this sandwich such as peanut and hazelnut butters. However, if you use the peanut butter, please avoid those brands with high fructose corn syrup and use the raw, all natural peanut butter. If you want to make it sweet, simply add a couple of teaspoons of agave nectar syrup.

NUTRITION FACTS

Based on a 2000 calorie diet per day

	Recipe Nutrition Per Serving	Daily Recommended Nutrition
Calories (kcal)	360	2000
Fat (g)	13	65
Saturated Fat (g)	1	20
Trans Fat (g)	0	
Poly Unsat Fat (g)	2	
Mono Unsat Fat (g)	6	
Cholesterol (mg)	0	300
Sodium (mg)	5	2400
Carbohydrates (g)	38	300
Dietary Fiber (g)	20	25
Total Sugars (g)	10	
Protein (g)	18	50
Vitamin A (IU)	0	5000
Vitamin C (mg)	0.1	60
Calcium (mg)	125	1000
Iron (mg)	7	18

Recipe Nutrition Per Serving

Daily Recommended Nutrition

Spicy Vinegar

Total Servings: 20
Serving Size: 1 tablespoon

Vinegar and peppers were a staple condiment in most restaurants in my hometown, and my mom and I used it frequently. We would pour this spicy vinegar over collard, mustard, or turnip greens prior to eating. This vinegar is so versatile and can also be used to make salad dressings or mixed in a stir-fry.

2 cups organic brown rice vinegar

15 whole Serrano peppers, rinsed and pat dry

2 cloves garlic, peeled and thinly sliced (optional)

1. Insert peppers into a clean bottle (about 16 ounces). If using garlic cloves, put inside the bottle after the peppers have been inserted.
2. Bring brown rice vinegar to a rolling boil in a small sauce pan; remove from heat and pour into the bottle using a funnel to prevent spillage. Close and let stand for at least a day before using.

Tidbits

The longer the vinegar sets, the more flavor is extracted from the peppers. This vinegar has a long shelf life and can be stored at room temperature.

Use any type of bottle; the recipe will change depending on the size. To measure the appropriate amount of vinegar needed, pour vinegar into the selected clean bottle prior to boiling.

NUTRITION FACTS

Based on a 2000 calorie diet per day

	Recipe Nutrition Per Serving	Daily Recommended Nutrition
Calories (kcal)	18	2000
Fat (g)	0	65
Saturated Fat (g)	0	20
Trans Fat (g)	0	
Poly Unsat Fat (g)	0	
Mono Unsat Fat (g)	0	
Cholesterol (mg)	0	300
Sodium (mg)	0.5	2400
Carbohydrates (g)	4	300
Dietary Fiber (g)	0.2	25
Total Sugars (g)	3	
Protein (g)	0.1	50
Vitamin A (IU)	43	5000
Vitamin C (mg)	2	60
Calcium (mg)	1	1000
Iron (mg)	0	18

Recipe Nutrition Per Serving

Daily Recommended Nutrition

Lemon Herb Oil

Total Servings: 24
Serving Size: 1 tablespoon

After being limited to just olive oil and balsamic vinegar, I wanted something different to drizzle over my salads. I love this oil because it reminds me of summer. This lemon herb oil is very light tasting and can be used for salads or as a marinade.

½ small lemon, rinsed and pat dry

2 sprigs dill, rinsed and pat dry

⅛ teaspoon finely ground Celtic Sea Salt® Brand

1½ cups grapeseed oil

1 tablespoon honey (optional)

1. Slice lemon into ¼-inch thick slices and remove any seeds. Insert lemon slices into a bottle (about 10 ounces). Bend the lemon slices slightly if the bottle opening is small; be careful not to tear the lemon.
2. Place the dill sprigs next to the bottle to determine the height required; if dill is too tall, trim the stems until correct height is achieved. Insert sprigs into the bottle.
3. Whisk salt and grapeseed oil in a bowl; pour oil into the bottle using a funnel. If using a smaller or larger bottle, adjust the amount of oil accordingly. (If using honey, whisk with the oil and salt before pouring into the bottle.)

Tidbits

Use a whole lemon (sliced) and 4 sprigs of dill for a more intense flavor. This oil should be stored in the refrigerator for at least a week.

To bring out more of the dill flavor, process all of the ingredients in a blender or food processor.

NUTRITION FACTS

Based on a 2000 calorie diet per day

	Recipe Nutrition Per Serving	Daily Recommended Nutrition
Calories (kcal)	121	2000
Fat (g)	14	65
Saturated Fat (g)	1	20
Trans Fat (g)	0	
Poly Unsat Fat (g)	10	
Mono Unsat Fat (g)	2	
Cholesterol (mg)	0	300
Sodium (mg)	9	2400
Carbohydrates (g)	0.1	300
Dietary Fiber (g)	0	25
Total Sugars (g)	0	
Protein (g)	0	50
Vitamin A (IU)	3	5000
Vitamin C (mg)	1	60
Calcium (mg)	0.4	1000
Iron (mg)	0	18

Recipe Nutrition Per Serving

Daily Recommended Nutrition

SIDE DISHES

Southern Style Cabbage

Total Servings: 5
Serving Size: 1 cup

I have very fond memories of eating cabbage mixed with crumbled pieces of cornbread. Green cabbage is one my favorite leafy green vegetables not only because of its taste, but also because it is very easy to prepare and quick to cook! After many tests, I have finally developed a recipe that has very similar flavors as traditional southern cabbage recipes, but without using smoked ham hocks and lard!

1 small green cabbage (about 2 pounds), rinsed

½ cup water

⅛ cup extra-virgin olive oil

2 teaspoons onion powder

¾ teaspoon Celtic Sea Salt® Brand

Pinch ground black pepper

1 Remove the outer leaves of the cabbage and cut into 8 quarters. Remove the core and cut cabbage into ½-inch wide strips.

2 Bring water to a boil in a small stockpot and add cabbage strips, oil, onion powder, salt and pepper. Reduce heat to medium and cook, covered, stirring often, about 15 to 20 minutes, or until desired tenderness. Be sure to pay attention to the cabbage to avoid scorching. Remove pot from the heat when done.

Tidbits

Cabbage can be prepared in a number of ways. However, the traditional Southern style cabbage is boiled with smoked meat and cooked until very soft. If desired, simply add ½ cup chopped smoked turkey leg and an additional cup of water to this recipe. Boil meat for about 30 minutes before adding cabbage. Typically smoked meat has lots of sodium, so if you have blood pressure issues, you will need to adjust the salt accordingly.

If you like the core, do not discard. Simply dice it into bite-size pieces and cook with the cabbage leaves.

NUTRITION FACTS

Based on a 2000 calorie diet per day

	Recipe Nutrition Per Serving	Daily Recommended Nutrition
Calories (kcal)	105	2000
Fat (g)	6	65
Saturated Fat (g)	1	20
Trans Fat (g)	0	
Poly Unsat Fat (g)	0.4	
Mono Unsat Fat (g)	4	
Cholesterol (mg)	0	300
Sodium (mg)	290	2400
Carbohydrates (g)	11	300
Dietary Fiber (g)	4	25
Total Sugars (g)	6	
Protein (g)	2	50
Vitamin A (IU)	0.5	5000
Vitamin C (mg)	60	91
Calcium (mg)	89	1000
Iron (mg)	1	18

Recipe Nutrition Per Serving

Daily Recommended Nutrition

Cornless Cornbread Dressing

Total Servings: 5
Serving Size: ¾ cup

For many years, Thanksgiving dinner was uneventful because I could not eat corn, which is the staple ingredient in cornbread dressing. I later learned about whole grain millet flour and became interested in using it as a cornmeal substitute in my dressing recipe because the color and texture were very similar to cornmeal. So, after baking a few unsuccessful batches, I finally created the right recipe that mimics my mother's cornbread dressing, even she was impressed!

2 cups finely chopped green onions

2 cups finely chopped celery

¾ cup plus 6 tablespoons water

⅛ cup plus 3 tablespoons olive oil

2 tablespoons ground flaxseeds

1 cup millet flour

1 cup brown rice flour

4 teaspoons baking powder

¼ teaspoon plus ⅛ teaspoon guar gum

2 tablespoons agave nectar syrup

¾ cup rice milk

2 teaspoons ground onion powder

⅛ teaspoon Celtic Sea Salt® Brand

1. Preheat the oven to 350°F. Bring ¾ cup of the water to a boil in a medium saucepan and add onions, celery and 3 tablespoons of the olive oil; cover and cook over low heat about 40 to 45 minutes. Remove from heat and let cool for 20 minutes.
2. Whisk ground flaxseeds and the remaining 6 tablespoons water in a small bowl; let stand for 2 to 3 minutes. The consistency should be similar to an egg that has been beaten.
3. Combine millet flour, rice flour, baking powder, guar gum, agave syrup, rice milk, the remaining ⅛ cup olive oil, and flaxseed mixture in a large bowl. Stir in the cooked seasoning, onion powder and salt with a large spoon until creamy and smooth.
4. Pour batter into an 8 x 8 glass baking dish. Bake on 350°F for 60 to 70 minutes. Use a toothpick to test for doneness. If no crumbs appear on the toothpick, remove dressing from oven. Let cool on a wire rack for 3 to 5 minutes.
5. Break bread into small bite-size pieces with a large spoon in the baking dish; the bread should have a very moist texture. Place dish back into the oven and bake for 8 to 10 minutes. Let bread cool for 5 to 10 minutes before serving.

Tidbit

There are many recipe variations for cornbread dressing; some are made with ground sage, chopped apples, raisins, or seafood. Create your own and follow this recipe as directed; be careful not to add too much extra liquid without increasing the amount of dry ingredients. It will definitely make a difference in the texture of this recipe.

NUTRITION FACTS

Based on a 2000 calorie diet per day

	Recipe Nutrition Per Serving	Daily Recommended Nutrition
Calories (kcal)	321	2000
Fat (g)	15	65
Saturated Fat (g)	2	20
Trans Fat (g)	0	
Poly Unsat Fat (g)	1	
Mono Unsat Fat (g)	9	
Cholesterol (mg)	0	300
Sodium (mg)	471	2400
Carbohydrates (g)	44	300
Dietary Fiber (g)	5	25
Total Sugars (g)	9	
Protein (g)	6	50
Vitamin A (IU)	2213	5000
Vitamin C (mg)	10	60
Calcium (mg)	131	1000
Iron (mg)	4	18

Southern Style Green Beans

Total Servings: 6
Serving Size: ½ cup

This is an old time classic in my neck of the woods that mom cooked quite often. I remember having green beans whenever she cooked rice and gravy with fried chicken. Of course, I have taken this classic southern recipe and made it just as delicious but a lot healthier. If you never liked green beans, this dish will give you a different perspective; so give this version a try.

¼ cup extra-virgin olive oil

¾ cup chopped onion

1 medium clove garlic

1 pound frozen (or fresh) cut green beans

2½ cups water

½ teaspoon plus ⅛ teaspoon Celtic Sea Salt® Brand

Pinch ground black pepper

1 tablespoon onion powder

⅛ teaspoon garlic powder

1 tablespoon agave nectar syrup

Heat oil in a large saucepan, over medium heat about 1 to 2 minutes. Add onions and garlic and stir, continually about 1 to 2 minutes. Add beans, water, salt, pepper, onion powder, garlic powder, and syrup, and cook, covered, over medium heat about 1 to 1½ hours, or until desired tenderness. (There should be very little water in the pot.)

Tidbits

When using fresh green beans, pick out the speckled beans, rinse and dry. Trim the ends (about ¼-inch down from both ends) and cut beans into 2 to 3-inch long pieces. Add an additional cup of water and cook over medium heat for an extra 30 minutes.

To really give these green beans a Southern spin, add 6 small boiling potatoes (rinsed and halved) or 1 cup chopped turnip roots (washed and peeled) during the last 15 to 20 minutes of the cook time.

NUTRITION FACTS

Based on a 2000 calorie diet per day

	Recipe Nutrition Per Serving	Daily Recommended Nutrition
Calories (kcal)	129	2000
Fat (g)	9	65
Saturated Fat (g)	1.3	20
Trans Fat (g)	0	
Poly Unsat Fat (g)	1	
Mono Unsat Fat (g)	7	
Cholesterol (mg)	0	300
Sodium (mg)	172	2400
Carbohydrates (g)	9	300
Dietary Fiber (g)	2.5	25
Total Sugars (g)	5	
Protein (g)	1	50
Vitamin A (IU)	90	5000
Vitamin C (mg)	6	60
Calcium (mg)	27	1000
Iron (mg)	0.4	18

Recipe Nutrition Per Serving

Daily Recommended Nutrition

Black-Eyed Peas

Total Servings: 6
Serving Size: ½ cup

Black-eyed peas are a soul food tradition typically eaten for New Year's dinner to symbolize good luck and prosperity. Holding to that tradition, every year, my mom would cook her black-eyed peas, greens and cornbread! I love eating these beans, despite the time of year, because they are tasty and they cook in less time in comparison to other beans!

2 cups dried black-eyed peas

2 quarts water (8 cups)

1 cup chopped onion

1 teaspoon Celtic Sea Salt® Brand

3 tablespoons onion powder

½ teaspoon garlic powder

3 tablespoons extra-virgin olive oil

2 teaspoons agave nectar syrup

¼ teaspoons ground black pepper

½ cup chopped okra (optional)

1. Discard any peas that are speckled or rotten. Add dried peas to a large bowl filled with 4 cups of the water. Let the peas soak for 1 to 2 hours. Drain the peas and rinse.
2. Transfer peas to a medium pot and add the remaining 4 cups water. Bring peas to a rolling boil; add onion, sea salt, onion and garlic powders, olive oil,agave syrup and black pepper and cook, covered, over medium heat until creamy, about 2 hours. If desired, add okra during the last 15 minutes of the cook time.

Tidbits

Frozen black-eyed peas can be used. There is no need to soak; reduce cook time to about 1 to 1½ hours. You can also use this recipe with dried lentils instead of the black-eyed peas.

To cream the peas, slightly open the lid of the pot and bring peas to a rolling boil. Continue to let the peas boil until they become soft and creamy. This may take about 10 to 15 minutes.

NUTRITION FACTS

Based on a 2000 calorie diet per day

	Recipe Nutrition Per Serving	Daily Recommended Nutrition
Calories (kcal)	208	2000
Fat (g)	7	65
Saturated Fat (g)	1	20
Trans Fat (g)	0	
Poly Unsat Fat (g)	0.6	
Mono Unsat Fat (g)	5.5	
Cholesterol (mg)	0	300
Sodium (mg)	297	2400
Carbohydrates (g)	35	300
Dietary Fiber (g)	15	25
Total Sugars (g)	4	
Protein (g)	13	50
Vitamin A (IU)	2	5000
Vitamin C (mg)	3	60
Calcium (mg)	43	1000
Iron (mg)	4	18

Recipe Nutrition Per Serving

Daily Recommended Nutrition

Steamed Veggies

Total Servings: 4
Serving Size: 1 cup

I had no idea how to prepare squash when I first purchased them because I never ate them as a child. However, I knew that I could not go wrong with steaming them. This recipe is quick, easy, and tasty, which makes it perfect for the busy person with little time to cook!

1½ cups sliced carrots, about ¼-inch thick

½ cup sliced sweet onions, peeled

3 medium zucchini (about 1½ pounds), sliced ¼-inch thick

3 medium yellow squash (about 1½ pounds), sliced ¼-inch thick

½ tablespoon fresh thyme leaves

2 tablespoons grapeseed oil

½ teaspoon Celtic Sea Salt® Brand

Pinch ground black pepper

1. Put carrots in top of double boiler and place over boiling water; upper pan should not touch water. Cover and steam, over medium-high heat about 5 to 7 minutes. Add in the following order: onion slices, zucchini, and yellow squash; cover and steam for an additional 3 to 5 minutes.
2. Remove steaming basket with the vegetables; transfer to a large bowl and gently toss with thyme, grapeseed oil, sea salt and pepper.

Tidbit

Since summer squash may be hard to find during the winter season, this recipe can be modified by substituting or adding other vegetables such as: broccoli florets, cauliflower florets, asparagus spears, bell peppers, as well as other herbs like rosemary, sage, etc.

NUTRITION FACTS

Based on a 2000 calorie diet per day

	Recipe Nutrition Per Serving	Daily Recommended Nutrition
Calories (kcal)	192	2000
Fat (g)	7	65
Saturated Fat (g)	0.7	20
Trans Fat (g)	0	
Poly Unsat Fat (g)	4.9	
Mono Unsat Fat (g)	1.1	
Cholesterol (mg)	0	300
Sodium (mg)	230	2400
Carbohydrates (g)	30	300
Dietary Fiber (g)	8	25
Total Sugars (g)	14	
Protein (g)	5	50
Vitamin A (IU)	21150	5000
Vitamin C (mg)	17	60
Calcium (mg)	91	1000
Iron (mg)	2	18

Recipe Nutrition Per Serving

Daily Recommended Nutrition

Mustard Greens

Total Servings: 4
Serving Size: 1 cup

Growing up, I remember my mom cooking her greens with some sort of cured pork meat such as ham hocks or pig tails. Since changing my diet, I have removed these from my recipe and made other substitutions to bring out more of the natural flavors of the mustard greens.

- 2 cups water
- 2 pounds frozen mustard greens
- ¾ teaspoon Celtic Sea Salt® Brand
- ¼ teaspoon agave nectar syrup
- ¼ cup extra-virgin olive oil
- ¾ cup chopped onion
- 4½ teaspoons onion powder
- ½ teaspoon spicy vinegar, see recipe (optional)

Bring water to a rolling boil in a large saucepan; add all of the ingredients. Reduce heat to medium and simmer, covered, until the greens are tender, about 25 to 30 minutes. (The cook time will vary based on how tender you like your greens.) If desired, serve with spicy vinegar.

Tidbits

Fresh mustard greens can also be used with this recipe. Be sure to cut off the stems and remove any bugs or damaged leaves, and wash the leaves in cool water, at least twice. Stack several leaves and roll, tightly; cut the leaves into ¼-inch strips and cook as instructed above.

If not vegetarian, substitute 1 cup of the water with 1 cup of low sodium chicken broth or add ½ cup chopped, smoked turkey leg, for even more flavor.

Try this recipe with other greens such as turnips, kale, and chard. Depending on desired tenderness, you may have to adjust the cook time.

NUTRITION FACTS

Based on a 2000 calorie diet per day

	Recipe Nutrition Per Serving	Daily Recommended Nutrition
Calories (kcal)	186	2000
Fat (g)	15	65
Saturated Fat (g)	2	20
Trans Fat (g)	0	
Poly Unsat Fat (g)	1	
Mono Unsat Fat (g)	11	
Cholesterol (mg)	0	300
Sodium (mg)	376	2400
Carbohydrates (g)	10	300
Dietary Fiber (g)	8.4	25
Total Sugars (g)	2	
Protein (g)	6	50
Vitamin A (IU)	11692	5000
Vitamin C (mg)	60	
Calcium (mg)	278	1000
Iron (mg)	3	18

Recipe Nutrition Per Serving

Daily Recommended Nutrition

Cornless Cornbread Muffins

Total Servings: 12
Serving Size: 2 muffins

This recipe is a twist on momma's cornbread recipe. Unlike her recipe, this one substitutes the cornmeal with gluten-free millet flour. I developed this recipe after receiving a list of potential inflammatory foods that I should avoid, which included corn. Cornless cornbread muffins are great for those who battle with arthritis. Trust me, you won't miss the cornmeal!

2 tablespoons ground flaxseeds

6 tablespoons water

1 cup millet flour

1 cup brown rice flour

4 teaspoons baking powder

⅛ teaspoon Celtic Sea Salt® Brand

¼ teaspoon plus ⅛ teaspoon guar gum

2 tablespoons agave nectar syrup

1¼ cups rice milk (or water)

¼ cup olive oil

1. Preheat the oven to 350°F. Whisk ground flaxseeds and water in a small bowl with a small wire whisk; let stand, about 2 to 3 minutes. The consistency should be similar to an egg that has been beaten.
2. Whisk millet flour, rice flour, baking powder, salt, guar gum, agave syrup, milk and oil in a large bowl with a large wire whisk. Stir in the flaxseed mixture and mix thoroughly until the batter is creamy and smooth; if too thick and difficult to stir, add an additional tablespoon of milk or water until the batter is easier to mix.
3. Pour the batter into a non-stick mini muffin pan, filling about three-fourths full; make sure that each section has equal amount of batter. Bake for 15 minutes, until the muffins are puffed and golden brown. If desired, use baking paper muffin cups for easy clean-up.

Tidbit

Any kind of bakeware can be used to bake these muffins, but the traditional pan that is most often used is the cast iron skillet. When using cast iron skillets, whether seasoned or unseasoned, coat with oil to prevent sticking.

If muffins are not golden brown on top, set the oven temperature to broil. Lightly brush the top of the muffins with about ¼ teaspoon olive oil and place back into the oven on the top rack. Broil until the top of the muffins achieves desired golden brown color, about 1 or 1 ½ minutes.

NUTRITION FACTS

Based on a 2000 calorie diet per day

	Recipe Nutrition Per Serving	Daily Recommended Nutrition
Calories (kcal)	142	2000
Fat (g)	6	65
Saturated Fat (g)	1	20
Trans Fat (g)	0	
Poly Unsat Fat (g)	0.3	
Mono Unsat Fat (g)	4	
Cholesterol (mg)	0	300
Sodium (mg)	200	2400
Carbohydrates (g)	20	300
Dietary Fiber (g)	2	25
Total Sugars (g)	3	
Protein (g)	2	50
Vitamin A (IU)	7	5000
Vitamin C (mg)	0	60
Calcium (mg)	18	1000
Iron (mg)	2	18

Candied Butternut Squash

Total Servings: 2
Serving Size: ½ cup

I didn't know what this funny looking squash was when I first saw it—it had a long neck, a round bottom and a hard exterior. After I figured out how to cook this bright orange delight, I was pleasantly surprised with the natural, sweet flavor of this winter squash. In fact, it reminded me of the sweet potato so I decided to prepare it in a similar way as my mother prepared candied yams. The cinnamon and syrup, makes this squash a delicious candied yam alternative!

1 pound butternut squash

4 teaspoons agave nectar syrup

¼ teaspoon cinnamon

Pinch ground cloves

1 Preheat the oven to 350°F. Peel butternut squash with a vegetable peeler and cut squash into ½-inch thick slices. Remove any seeds and strings with a spoon. Put squash onto a baking sheet lined with parchment paper (or aluminum foil) and bake about 40 to 50 minutes. Place the baking sheet on to a cooling rack; let cool about 5 to 8 minutes.

2 Add syrup, cinnamon, and cloves to a small saucepan and stir with a small spoon until well mixed. Simmer, uncovered over low heat 1 to 2 minutes; add butternut squash slices and coat with the syrup mixture.

Tidbit

For a savory vegetable side dish, replace the syrup, cinnamon and cloves with ½ teaspoon extra-virgin olive oil and 2 teaspoons chopped fresh or dried sage leaves. Bake, uncovered, for 40 to 50 minutes, or until desired tenderness.

NUTRITION FACTS

Based on a 2000 calorie diet per day

	Recipe Nutrition Per Serving	Daily Recommended Nutrition
Calories (kcal)	82	2000
Fat (g)	0.1	65
Saturated Fat (g)	.02	20
Trans Fat (g)	0	
Poly Unsat Fat (g)	.04	
Mono Unsat Fat (g)	.01	
Cholesterol (mg)	0	300
Sodium (mg)	4	2400
Carbohydrates (g)	22	300
Dietary Fiber (g)	4	25
Total Sugars (g)	12	
Protein (g)	1	50
Vitamin A (IU)	11435	5000
Vitamin C (mg)	16	60
Calcium (mg)	46	1000
Iron (mg)	1	18

Red Beans

Total Servings: 8
Serving Size: ½ cup

Red beans and rice was definitely a weekly meal in my house and no matter how often I ate them, I would still get excited whenever my mom served these beans with fried chicken!

- 1¾ cups dried red kidney beans
- 2 quarts water (about 8 cups)
- 1 cup chopped onion
- 1 clove garlic, minced
- 3 tablespoons onion powder
- 1 teaspoon Celtic Sea Salt® Brand
- ¼ cup extra-virgin olive oil
- 1½ teaspoons honey
- ½ teaspoon ground sage
- ½ teaspoon red pepper flakes
- ⅛ teaspoon celery seeds
- Dash ground black pepper
- ½ cup chopped smoked turkey (optional)

1. Inspect the beans and discard the ones with holes or spots; add beans to a large bowl filled with 3 cups of the water; soak beans in the refrigerator about 8 hours or overnight. Drain beans and rinse.
2. Bring to a boil the remaining 5 cups water and the remaining ingredients in a small stockpot. If desired, add smoked turkey. Reduce to medium-low heat and simmer, covered, until beans are tender and creamy, stirring occasionally, about 1½ to 2 hours. (A slow cooker can be used; just cook beans on low, until the desired tenderness and creaminess, about 8 to 10 hours.)

Tidbits

To cream the beans, slightly open the lid of the pot and bring beans to a rolling boil. Continue to let the beans boil until they become soft and creamy. This may take an additional 10 to 15 minutes after the beans become tender.

There are different brands of red kidney beans—some brands cook in shorter times and are soft and creamy, while others cook longer and are firmer. Depending on the brand, you may have to add more water and allow the beans to cook longer before they get creamy.

NUTRITION FACTS

Based on a 2000 calorie diet per day

	Recipe Nutrition Per Serving	Daily Recommended Nutrition
Calories (kcal)	210	2000
Fat (g)	7	65
Saturated Fat (g)	1	20
Trans Fat (g)	0	
Poly Unsat Fat (g)	1	
Mono Unsat Fat (g)	6	
Cholesterol (mg)	0	300
Sodium (mg)	219	2400
Carbohydrates (g)	25	300
Dietary Fiber (g)	10	25
Total Sugars (g)	4	
Protein (g)	10	50
Vitamin A (IU)	54	5000
Vitamin C (mg)	4	60
Calcium (mg)	61	1000
Iron (mg)	3	18

Brown Rice

Total Servings: 2
Serving Size: ½ cup

Brown rice definitely took a lot of mental preparation in order for me to give up white rice! However, once I learned that the healthy nutrients have been stripped away from the natural brown rice and polished white, I knew that I had to learn to eat brown rice. It took a few tries for me to cook perfect brown rice—it was either too hard or mushy. But after lots of trial and error, I finally got the right method. So, if you had similar experiences of under cooking or over cooking brown rice, don't give up; instead try this recipe—it works every time!

½ cup uncooked long-grain brown rice

½ cup water

¼ teaspoon Celtic Sea Salt® Brand (optional)

¼ teaspoon turmeric (optional)

1 Place the rice in a fine mesh strainer set over a bowl. Rinse under running water, swishing rice with hands. Drain thoroughly. Continue until the water is clear, no longer brown.

2 Add rice and water to a small saucepan and bring to a boil over high heat. (If using salt and turmeric, add during this step.) Reduce heat to low; cook, covered until the rice is tender and the water is fully absorbed, about 50 to 60 minutes. Let stand, covered, about 5 minutes to 10 minutes. With a fork, gently lift the rice to fluff before serving.

Tidbits

The key tip for cooking perfect rice, is to make sure that you use equal parts water and rice—i.e. 2 cups water and 2 cups rice. If you want the rice a little stickier/softer, then just add more water. This recipe will work for other varieties of whole grain rice.

Brown rice is a whole grain and is more nutritious than the highly refined white rice. Unlike the natural brown rice, white rice has been processed with the outer layers (the bran and germ) of the whole grain removed.

NUTRITION FACTS

Based on a 2000 calorie diet per day

	Recipe Nutrition Per Serving	Daily Recommended Nutrition
Calories (kcal)	108	2000
Fat (g)	1	65
Saturated Fat (g)	0.2	20
Trans Fat (g)	0	
Poly Unsat Fat (g)	0.3	
Mono Unsat Fat (g)	0.3	
Cholesterol (mg)	0	300
Sodium (mg)	5	2400
Carbohydrates (g)	22	300
Dietary Fiber (g)	2	25
Total Sugars (g)	0.3	
Protein (g)	3	50
Vitamin A (IU)	0	5000
Vitamin C (mg)	0	60
Calcium (mg)	10	1000
Iron (mg)	0.4	18

Recipe Nutrition Per Serving

Daily Recommended Nutrition

Quinoa

Total Servings: 4
Serving Size: ½ cup

As I browsed the internet looking for gluten-free foods, I found quinoa (keen-wah) and was intrigued, not just by the fact that it is an excellent source of protein, but also because of the name—I had no idea how to pronounce it! When I started cooking quinoa, I destroyed several batches! I had no idea how to cook these tiny seeds—it was either too mushy or too hard! So, after a few mishaps, I was able to finally cook quinoa to perfection—light and fluffy. Not only does this grain have excellent nutritional value, but also it cooks in less than 20 minutes! If you are tired of eating brown rice and potatoes and want something different, give this recipe a try.

1 cup uncooked quinoa

1 cup water (or vegetable stock)

¼ teaspoon Celtic Sea Salt® Brand (optional)

¼ teaspoon turmeric (optional)

1 Place the quinoa in a fine mesh strainer set over a bowl. Rinse under running water, swishing quinoa with your hands. Drain completely. Continue until the water is clear, no longer brown.

2 Bring the quinoa and water to a boil in a small saucepan over high heat. (If using salt and turmeric, add during this step.) Reduce the heat to low and cook, covered until the water is fully absorbed, about 15 to 17 minutes. Let stand, covered, about 5 minutes to 10 minutes. With a fork, gently lift the quinoa to fluff before serving.

Tidbits

Quinoa is not a true grain, but is cooked and eaten as a grain. It has a light fluffy texture and is easy to digest than grains.

Quinoa is very versatile and can be eaten in a similar manner as rice; it also tastes great in almost any salad!

NUTRITION FACTS

Based on a 2000 calorie diet per day

Nutrient	Recipe Nutrition Per Serving	Daily Recommended Nutrition
Calories (kcal)	121	2000
Fat (g)	2	65
Saturated Fat (g)	0	20
Trans Fat (g)	0	
Poly Unsat Fat (g)	0	
Mono Unsat Fat (g)	0	
Cholesterol (mg)	0	300
Sodium (mg)	8	2400
Carbohydrates (g)	23	300
Dietary Fiber (g)	2	25
Total Sugars (g)	0	
Protein (g)	5	50
Vitamin A (IU)	0	5000
Vitamin C (mg)	0	60
Calcium (mg)	15	1000
Iron (mg)	3	18

Recipe Nutrition Per Serving

Daily Recommended Nutrition

MEAT & VEGETARIAN ENTREES

Oven-Fried Chicken Wings

Total Servings: 8
Serving Size: 1 wing

In my house, we ate fried chicken almost everyday! This recipe was created to satisfy my cravings for fried chicken, but without actually frying the chicken. Savory, juicy, crispy and golden brown best describe this chicken recipe. It is considered as the best alternative to the infamous fried chicken! This oven-baked delight has the appearance of fried chicken with less fat. Both kids and adults love these wings!

8 whole chicken wings (about 1½ pounds), rinsed and cleaned (remove hair)

½ cup brown rice flour

½ cup quinoa flour

1 teaspoon guar gum

2 teaspoons garlic powder

1 tablespoon onion powder

¼ teaspoon Celtic Sea Salt® Brand

⅛ teaspoon nutmeg

⅛ teaspoon ground white pepper

¼ teaspoon ground sage

¼ teaspoon plus ⅛ teaspoon paprika

2 tablespoons olive oil

1. Preheat the oven to 350°F. Add brown rice flour, quinoa flour, and guar gum to a plastic storage bag. Grease the rack of a roasting pan with 1 tablespoon of the olive oil using a basting brush (or use a baking sheet with a greased cooling rack placed on top of the pan; this will allow the chicken drippings to fall to bottom of pan.) Line the bottom with aluminum foil for easy clean-up.

2. Fold the chicken wing tip underneath the drum portion (the biggest part of the wing); this will form a triangle shape. Mix chicken, garlic powder, onion powder, sea salt, nutmeg, white pepper, sage and paprika in a large bowl by hand until all pieces have been coated with the seasoning. Rinse hands immediately in warm, soapy water to avoid cross contamination.

3. Place 3 or 4 seasoned wings into the storage bag that contains the flour mixture; seal and shake the bag to coat each wing with the flour. Remove wings from the bag, shake off the excess flour, and place onto the greased roasting pan; continue until all wings have been coated with flour. Baste wings with the remaining tablespoon of olive oil using a basting brush and bake for 1 hour. Turn the wings with tongs and bake on the other side, until crispy, about 10 to 15 minutes. Turn the wings once more and bake, until crispy, golden brown, about 10 to 15 minutes.

Tidbit

This recipe can be used with other chicken parts (breast, legs and thighs). However, to reduce the amount of fat and calories, remove the skin first. Try this recipe with skinless thighs; this will be a 50% reduction in calories, fat and sodium in comparison to one chicken wing.

NUTRITION FACTS

Based on a 2000 calorie diet per day

	Recipe Nutrition Per Serving	Daily Recommended Nutrition
Calories (kcal)	287	2000
Fat (g)	19	65
Saturated Fat (g)	5.3	20
Trans Fat (g)	0	
Poly Unsat Fat (g)	0.1	
Mono Unsat Fat (g)	1	
Cholesterol (mg)	105	300
Sodium (mg)	105	2400
Carbohydrates (g)	12	300
Dietary Fiber (g)	2	25
Total Sugars (g)	.01	
Protein (g)	17	50
Vitamin A (IU)	41	5000
Vitamin C (mg)	0.2	60
Calcium (mg)	6.7	1000
Iron (mg)	1	18

Blackened Wild Salmon

Total Servings: 2
Serving Size: 4 ounces

I have grown to love wild salmon. I started eating this pinkish-orange color fish because of its wonderful nutritional properties. Salmon is indeed in a class by itself in terms of its flavor, but when cooked in different ways it offers a variety of flavors. My favorite way to eat this distinct fish is blackened and pan-fried.

½ pound wild salmon fillet (about ½-inch thick), rinsed and pat dry

¼ teaspoon Celtic Sea Salt® Brand

1 teaspoon ground black pepper

1 tablespoon extra-virgin olive oil (or lemon herb oil see recipe)

1 Heat the oil in a large skillet over medium-high heat, about 2 to 3 minutes. Season one side of the salmon evenly with salt and black pepper.

2 Place salmon, seasoned side down, in the skillet. Reduce heat slightly and cook about 3 to 5 minutes. Turn the fish with a wide spatula and cook the other side, about 3 to 5 minutes, or until opaque throughout. Remove salmon from skillet and let stand for 1 to 2 minutes before serving. (Sometimes the fish will stick to the bottom of the pan if not enough oil so be careful to avoid tearing.)

Tidbits

Depending on the type of skillet and the temperature of the skillet the fish may stick to the pan thus making it difficult to turn. In this case, add more oil or simply reduce the heat and cook, covered. (Note that when the skillet is covered, the fish may not have that "blackened" effect due to the moisture created when the skillet is covered.)

Typically the salmon that comes from the Pacific Ocean is wild caught and does not contain any antibiotics, synthetic coloring agents or growth hormones, unlike most salmon from the Atlantic Ocean, which many times are farm-raised.

NUTRITION FACTS

Based on a 2000 calorie diet per day

	Recipe Nutrition Per Serving	Daily Recommended Nutrition
Calories (kcal)	224	2000
Fat (g)	14	65
Saturated Fat (g)	2	20
Trans Fat (g)	0	
Poly Unsat Fat (g)	8	
Mono Unsat Fat (g)	4	
Cholesterol (mg)	62	300
Sodium (mg)	255	2400
Carbohydrates (g)	1	300
Dietary Fiber (g)	0.3	25
Total Sugars (g)	.01	
Protein (g)	23	50
Vitamin A (IU)	49	5000
Vitamin C (mg)	0.2	60
Calcium (mg)	18	1000
Iron (mg)	1	18

Recipe Nutrition Per Serving

Daily Recommended Nutrition

Cod with Pesto and Rice

Total Servings: 2
Serving Size: 4 ounce fillet, 1 cup rice

I created this beautiful and tasty recipe by accident! I was trying to blacken the cod, but it was so delicate that it started separating into small chunks! So I decided to place the chunks of fish on top of the rice dish to make it look fancy. This is a very quick and easy dish to prepare and simply delicious. The pairing of the delicate flavor of cod with the buttery-like taste of the pesto is outstanding!

2 cups cooked brown rice (see recipe)

½ cup pesto (see recipe)

1¼ cups frozen green peas

¼ teaspoon lemon zest

½ teaspoon Celtic Sea Salt® Brand

½ pound wild cod fillets, rinsed and pat dry

1 teaspoon ground black pepper

1 tablespoon grapeseed oil

1 tablespoon water

¼ teaspoon paprika (optional garnish)

1. Prepare the rice and pesto.
2. Heat a large skillet over low heat for 1 to 2 minutes; add pesto, rice, peas, lemon zest and ¼ teaspoon of the salt; stir often with a large spoon until the rice and peas have been coated with the pesto. Simmer, covered, about 5 to 7 minutes. Peas should still have its bright green color.
3. Season both sides of the fish with the remaining ¼ teaspoon salt and pepper. Heat oil in a different skillet over high heat about 2 to 3 minutes; add fish. Reduce heat slightly and cook for 3 to 5 minutes. Turn the fish with a wide spatula and cook the second side about 3 to 5 minutes, or until opaque throughout. Remove fish and place into a dish, covered, about 4 to 5 minutes. Separate the cod into smaller pieces using a fork.
4. Transfer pesto rice onto a large serving plate and place the small cod pieces on top of the rice. If desired, sprinkle paprika on top for garnish.

Tidbits

Be careful not to cook peas too long to avoid losing the vibrant green color.

If you are allergic to fish, substitute with chicken and follow the recipe as instructed.

NUTRITION FACTS

Based on a 2000 calorie diet per day

Nutrient	Recipe Nutrition Per Serving	Daily Recommended Nutrition
Calories (kcal)	546	2000
Fat (g)	21	65
Saturated Fat (g)	3	20
Trans Fat (g)	0	
Poly Unsat Fat (g)	6	
Mono Unsat Fat (g)	11	
Cholesterol (mg)	42	300
Sodium (mg)	536	2400
Carbohydrates (g)	57	300
Dietary Fiber (g)	8	25
Total Sugars (g)	5	
Protein (g)	31	50
Vitamin A (IU)	660	5000
Vitamin C (mg)	10	60
Calcium (mg)	44	1000
Iron (mg)	3	18

Pot Roast

Total Servings: 8
Serving Size: ½-inch thick slice

My momma's pot roast was alway delicious. Though she would use a few shortcuts to help her create that perfect flavor, it was good every time! This is definitely not my momma's recipe, but it is truly a close runner-up. The roast and gravy in this recipe is just as tender and mouth-watering as I remembered as a little girl.

2 pounds chuck roast, rinsed

¾ cup chopped onion

1 large clove garlic, minced

3½ tablepsoons onion powder

1¾ teaspoons garlic powder

¼ teaspoon thyme leaves

¼ teaspoon chopped rosemary leaves

1¼ teaspoons Celtic Sea Salt® Brand

2½ cups water

2 tablespoons olive oil

3 tablespoons tapioca flour

1 tablespoon gluten free, all-purpose flour

1 medium bay leaf

1. Add ½ cup of the onions, garlic, onion powder, garlic powder, thyme, rosemary, salt and 2 cups of the water to a 5-quart oval slow cooker.
2. Mix the remaining ½ cup water and the tapioca flour with a wire whisk in a small bowl; add tapioca mixture to the slow cooker, stirring continually, until well mixed. Place the roast into the slow cooker and cook, covered, over high heat, until the meat is fork-tender, and easy to separate with a fork, about 4 hours. Reduce heat to low/warm, and simmer, covered, until gravy is prepared, about 30 minutes.
3. Preheat oil in a wide, large saucepan over medium-high heat; add the remaining chopped onions and cook, stirring continually, until onions start to turn slightly brown, about 1 or 2 minutes. Reduce heat to medium and add flour, stirring often until flour becomes a caramel or golden brown color, with no flour lumps, about 3 to 4 minutes. (This will become the base for the gravy.) Whisk in 3 cups of the pot roast broth, slowly, stirring constantly, until the flour mixture (also known as roux) is well combined and smooth. Add bay leaf and pot roast to the gravy and simmer, covered, stirring occasionally, about 10 to 15 minutes.

Tidbit

The required cook time is dependent on the slow cooker brand type. Some brands cook foods really fast and others cook relatively slow, so you may need to adjust the cook time. Review your slow cooker manual prior to starting.

NUTRITION FACTS

Based on a 2000 calorie diet per day

	Recipe Nutrition Per Serving	Daily Recommended Nutrition
Calories (kcal)	207	2000
Fat (g)	8	65
Saturated Fat (g)	2	20
Trans Fat (g)	0	
Poly Unsat Fat (g)	0.5	
Mono Unsat Fat (g)	5	
Cholesterol (mg)	50	300
Sodium (mg)	394	2400
Carbohydrates (g)	5	300
Dietary Fiber (g)	1	25
Total Sugars (g)	1	
Protein (g)	26	50
Vitamin A (IU)	8	5000
Vitamin C (mg)	2	60
Calcium (mg)	32	1000
Iron (mg)	2	18

Recipe Nutrition Per Serving

Daily Recommended Nutrition

Turkey Spaghetti

Total Servings: 12
Serving Size: 1 cup

Who doesn't like spaghetti? Spaghetti and meatballs was a popular meal for my family, especially for my brother—it was the first meal that he learned to cook and he ate it religiously! This modified recipe has been a favorite of many of my friends, even though they didn't know that it was gluten-free!

$2\frac{1}{2}$ pounds ground turkey

4 tablespoons extra-virgin olive oil

2 cups chopped onions

2 cloves garlic, minced

4 teaspoons garlic powder

$2\frac{1}{2}$ tablespoons onion powder

2 teaspoons ground sage

2 tablespoons ground oregano

1 teaspoon crushed red pepper flakes

$\frac{3}{4}$ teaspoon Celtic Sea Salt® Brand

$\frac{1}{4}$ teaspoon Stevia

16 ounces uncooked brown rice spaghetti

$1\frac{1}{2}$ tablespoons honey

2 (25.5 ounce) jars Muir Glen Pasta Sauce

1. Heat a large skillet with 2 tablespoons of the oil over medium heat about 1 to 2 minutes. Add onions and garlic; cook and stir often for 2 to 3 minutes. (The onions and garlic will start to turn brown.) Add ground turkey, breaking up the meat with a large spoon, until no longer pink, about 5 to 6 minutes. Add garlic and onion powders, sage, oregano, red pepper flakes, salt and stevia, and cook, stirring often, about 1 to 2 minutes. Stir in the honey and pasta sauce and simmer, covered, over low heat; until needed.

2. Meanwhile, bring 4 quarts water to a boil in a large stock pot. Stir in the spaghetti and the remaining 2 tablespoons olive oil, and cook, stirring often, about 8 to 10 minutes. Drain the noodles and rinse in a colander under cold water until cool. Add the noodles to the meat sauce, and continue to simmer, covered, stirring often, about 3 to 5 minutes.

Tidbits

Spaghetti absorbs a lot of the meat sauce as it continues to cool. If you are not serving this meal immediately, use only 12 ounces uncooked spaghetti ($\frac{3}{4}$ of the bag).

This recipe is great for freezing; just double the recipe and freeze the extra pasta and sauce separately. Make sure the noodles are dry before placing into the freezer bags. Be advised that when freezing brown rice pasta, it must be cooked al dente (about 3 to 5 minutes) to avoid it becoming very soft (mushy) during the defrost process.

NUTRITION FACTS

Based on a 2000 calorie diet per day

	Recipe Nutrition Per Serving	Daily Recommended Nutrition
Calories (kcal)	343	2000
Fat (g)	5	65
Saturated Fat (g)	0.4	20
Trans Fat (g)	0	
Poly Unsat Fat (g)	0.2	
Mono Unsat Fat (g)	2	
Cholesterol (mg)	38	300
Sodium (mg)	516	2400
Carbohydrates (g)	47	300
Dietary Fiber (g)	4	25
Total Sugars (g)	8	
Protein (g)	29	50
Vitamin A (IU)	855	5000
Vitamin C (mg)	9	60
Calcium (mg)	48	1000
Iron (mg)	4	18

Recipe Nutrition Per Serving

Daily Recommended Nutrition

Quinoa and Chicken

Total Servings: 3
Serving Size: ½ cup

I always look for opportunities to add variety to my list of dinner options. One day, all I had in the fridge were cooked quinoa, frozen chicken and lots of vegetables. So, I decided to put these items together to create a quick and easy meal and it turned out great!

1 cup cooked quinoa (see recipe)

1 ounce boneless, skinless chicken tenders (about 2 tenders), rinsed and cubed

2 tablespoons extra-virgin olive oil

¾ cup chopped onion

2 tablespoons chopped leeks (or green onions), white part of bulb only

½ medium red bell pepper (about 2-inch round), sliced and seeded

1 clove garlic, minced

½ medium green bell pepper (about 2-inch round), sliced and seeded

½ teaspoon Celtic Sea Salt® Brand

1 tablespoon onion powder

⅛ teaspoon garlic powder

¼ cup chopped fresh basil

⅛ teaspoon paprika (optional)

1. Prepare quinoa.
2. Heat 1 tablespoon of the oil and onions in a large skillet over medium-high heat, about 1 to 2 minutes; reduce the heat to medium-low, add chicken and ¼ teaspoon of the salt and cook, stirring often, until done (no pink), about 5 to 7 minutes. Add leeks, garlic and bell pepper slices and cook, covered, about 2 to 3 minutes.
3. Stir in the cooked quinoa, the remaining tablespoon olive oil, onion powder, garlic powder and the remaining ¼ teaspoon salt and simmer, covered, over low heat about 2 to 3 minutes. Remove from heat and let stand about 2 minutes, or until cool; stir in the chopped basil. If desired, sprinkle paprika for garnish.

Tidbit

Do not add basil to the quinoa during the cooking process because the basil will wilt and become black quickly.

NUTRITION FACTS

Based on a 2000 calorie diet per day

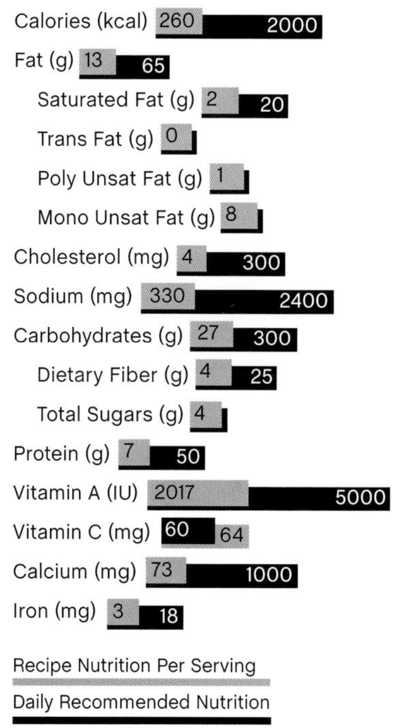

Simple Veggie Chow Mein

Total Servings: 2½
Serving Size: 1 cup

One day I craved chow mein from one of my favorite Chinese restaurants, but I knew that I couldn't eat it because it was cooked with soy and wheat noodles. To satisfy my cravings, I re-created this Chinese classic and made it just as delicious without wheat and soy!

2 tablespoons olive oil

¼ cup chopped onion

1 clove garlic, minced

1½ cups frozen (or fresh) stir-fry vegetables

¼ teaspoon Celtic Sea Salt® Brand

½ tablespoon onion powder

½ teaspoon finely grated ginger

½ tablespoon balsamic vinegar (or soy sauce)

⅛ teaspoon agave syrup

¼ cup water

2 ounces uncooked brown rice fettuccine pasta (or any whole grain pasta)

1 tablespoon sliced green onions, green part only (optional)

1. Heat 1 tablespoon of the olive oil in a large skillet (or wok) about 1 to 2 minutes; add chopped onion and cook over medium heat about 2 to 3 minutes. Add mixed vegetables, salt, and onion powder and cook, covered, over medium-low heat, about 8 to 10 minutes. If using fresh vegetables, the cook time will vary depending on the type. Just cook until your desired tenderness.
2. Bring 4 quarts water to a boil in a large stock pot. Stir in the pasta and the remaining tablespoon olive oil, and cook, stirring often, about 8 to 10 minutes. Drain the noodles and rinse in a colander under cold water until cool.
3. Add cooked pasta, ginger, balsamic vinegar, agave syrup and water to the skillet with the cooked vegetables and stir until well mixed. Simmer, covered, about 3 to 5 minutes. If desired, before serving top with green onions for garnish.

Tidbits

The balsamic vinegar is added for color. For the traditional chow mien flavor, use 1 tablespoon of low sodium soy sauce instead of balsamic vinegar. Soy sauce is salty, so you may have to adjust the amount of salt.

Roasted sesame oil will also give this recipe a twist; however, use sparingly as it is strong in flavor. If desired use ½ tablespoon each of olive oil and sesame oil.

NUTRITION FACTS

Based on a 2000 calorie diet per day

	Recipe Nutrition Per Serving	Daily Recommended Nutrition
Calories (kcal)	168	2000
Fat (g)	6	65
Saturated Fat (g)	1	20
Trans Fat (g)	0	
Poly Unsat Fat (g)	1	
Mono Unsat Fat (g)	4	
Cholesterol (mg)	0	300
Sodium (mg)	196	2400
Carbohydrates (g)	23	300
Dietary Fiber (g)	3	25
Total Sugars (g)	2	
Protein (g)	3	50
Vitamin A (IU)	600	5000
Vitamin C (mg)	16	60
Calcium (mg)	24	1000
Iron (mg)	1	18

Veggie Spaghetti Squash

Total Servings: 4
Serving Size: ½ cup

I watched one of my favorite celebrity chefs cook spaghetti squash and I was intrigued by this strange looking squash so I decided to give it a try. Spaghetti squash is so interesting to me because it has the look of spaghetti when cooked without the extra calories, which is always good in my book!

2 pounds spaghetti squash (1 medium)

1 tablespoon olive oil

2 tablespoons chopped onions

½ red bell pepper (about 2-inch round), sliced and seeded

1 cup chopped fresh broccoli florets

½ cup chopped fresh cauliflower florets

½ cup diced fresh carrots

1 tablespoon chopped leeks

1 teaspoon granulated onion powder

½ teaspoon Celtic Sea Salt® Brand

1. Preheat the oven to 350°F. Place the squash onto a baking sheet and bake for 1 hour 10 minutes. Transfer to a wire cooling rack and let squash cool about 5 to 10 minutes.
2. Cut the cooked squash in half, lengthwise, and remove the seeds using a spoon and discard. Scrape the flesh into a large bowl, separating into strands with a fork. As you scrape, the squash will start to release and look like long thin spaghetti.
3. Heat a large skillet over medium heat for 1 to 2 minutes. Add olive oil and onions, stirring often, about 1 to 2 minutes. Stir in the bell pepper, broccoli, cauliflower, carrots and leeks; reduce heat to low and cook, covered, until desired tenderness, about 15 to 20 minutes. Stir in the spaghetti squash, granulated onion powder, and salt and simmer, covered, about 5 to 7 minutes.

Tidbit

Spaghetti squash tastes great with a variety of sauces, especially tomato sauce. The next time you cook spaghetti with meatsauce (see recipe), substitute the pasta with spaghetti squash.

NUTRITION FACTS

Based on a 2000 calorie diet per day

	Recipe Nutrition Per Serving	Daily Recommended Nutrition
Calories (kcal)	87	2000
Fat (g)	4	65
Saturated Fat (g)	1	20
Trans Fat (g)	0	
Poly Unsat Fat (g)	0.5	
Mono Unsat Fat (g)	3	
Cholesterol (mg)	0	300
Sodium (mg)	242	2400
Carbohydrates (g)	12	300
Dietary Fiber (g)	4	25
Total Sugars (g)	5	
Protein (g)	2	50
Vitamin A (IU)	6301	5000
Vitamin C (mg)	63	60
Calcium (mg)	44	1000
Iron (mg)	1	18

DESSERTS & DRINKS

Apple Cinnamon Minis

Total Servings: 8
Serving Size: 3 mini muffins

A friend once said after eating my apple cinnamon muffins, "I can't believe that these do not have butter and eggs; they're so light!" I get this sort of comment quite often from many people who taste these muffins. These wonderful, delicious pastries are great for breakfast, dessert, or whenever you want something sweet. This recipe is a must try, you will be pleasantly surprised.

1 tablespoon ground flaxseeds

3 tablespoons water

1 cup gluten-free all-purpose flour (or whole wheat or spelt flour)

⅛ teaspoon Celtic Sea Salt® Brand

2 teaspoons baking powder

2 teaspoons cinnamon

¼ cup chopped pecans

½ cup unsweetened applesauce

2 teaspoons vanilla extract

½ cup raw agave nectar syrup

¼ cup olive oil

1. Preheat the oven to 330°F. Whisk ground flaxseeds and water in a small bowl; let stand about 2 to 3 minutes. The consistency should be similar to an egg that has been beaten.
2. Add flour, salt, baking powder, and 1½ teaspoons of the cinnamon to a medium bowl and mix with a small spoon. In a different bowl, mix the pecans and the remaining ½ teaspoon cinnamon with a spoon. Set both bowls aside until ready for use.
3. Mix the applesauce, vanilla extract, agave nectar syrup, olive oil and the flaxseed mixture in a large bowl on low speed using a handheld mixer (or free standing mixer), about 1 to 2 minutes; slowly add the flour mixture and mix, about 1 to 2 minutes. Do not over mix. Pour batter evenly into a non-stick 24-cup mini muffin pan (or paper muffin molds); top with the seasoned pecans and bake about 15 to 18 minutes.

Tidbits

The bake time and temperature will vary depending on the pan size. For pans with deeper cups, reduce the temperature and bake longer. Use a cake tester or toothpick to test for doneness. If no crumbs appear on the toothpick, then the muffin is done.

For a lighter, summer dessert, add ½ cup fresh blueberries, ½ teaspoon lemon extract (reduce vanilla extract to 1½ teaspoons) and substitute the olive oil with grapeseed oil. Follow as instructed above.

NUTRITION FACTS

Based on a 2000 calorie diet per day

	Recipe Nutrition Per Serving	Daily Recommended Nutrition
Calories (kcal)	164	2000
Fat (g)	10	65
Saturated Fat (g)	1	20
Trans Fat (g)	0	
Poly Unsat Fat (g)	1	
Mono Unsat Fat (g)	7	
Cholesterol (mg)	0	300
Sodium (mg)	174	2400
Carbohydrates (g)	20	300
Dietary Fiber (g)	2	25
Total Sugars (g)	17	
Protein (g)	1	50
Vitamin A (IU)	9	5000
Vitamin C (mg)	0.1	60
Calcium (mg)	20	1000
Iron (mg)	1	18

Recipe Nutrition Per Serving

Daily Recommended Nutrition

Apples á la Mode

Total Servings: 2
Serving Size: ½ cup

I love apple pie á la mode and anything else served á la mode style—simply put, I love anything served with ice cream! Since removing wheat from my diet, I struggled to find desserts, so after craving apple pie, I decided to make my version of a no-crust apple pie á la mode that's not only yummy, but also low in calories. If you love apple pie á la mode, then you have to try this recipe.

2 medium gala apples, rinsed and peeled

¼ teaspoon cinnamon

⅛ teaspoon nutmeg

⅛ teaspoon ground cloves

⅛ teaspoon stevia

1 tablespoon agave nectar syrup

3 tablespoons water

1 scoop non-dairy ice cream (about ½ cup)

1. Cut apples into quarters and remove the stem and core; chop apples into small cubes.
2. Add apples, cinnamon, nutmeg, cloves, stevia, agave syrup, and water to a small saucepan and cook, covered, over medium heat, until the apples are tender (soft), about 40 to 45 minutes. Use a fork to pierce the apples to determine if the apples are at the desired tenderness. Be sure that the apples are not too soft then it will become applesauce. Serve apples in a bowl or martini glass, topped with ice cream.

Tidbits

The type of apples used in this recipe is important because of the different levels of sweetness. In my opinion, Fuji and gala are two of the sweetest apples. If you like very sweet desserts, add an extra tablespoon of syrup.

This recipe is versatile and can be used with other fruits such as pears, peaches and figs!

NUTRITION FACTS

Based on a 2000 calorie diet per day

	Recipe Nutrition Per Serving	Daily Recommended Nutrition
Calories (kcal)	201	2000
Fat (g)	3	65
Saturated Fat (g)	0.3	20
Trans Fat (g)	0	
Poly Unsat Fat (g)	0.1	
Mono Unsat Fat (g)	.01	
Cholesterol (mg)	0	300
Sodium (mg)	52	2400
Carbohydrates (g)	45	300
Dietary Fiber (g)	6	25
Total Sugars (g)	35	
Protein (g)	0.5	50
Vitamin A (IU)	149	5000
Vitamin C (mg)	9	60
Calcium (mg)	24	1000
Iron (mg)	1	18

Spicy Carrot Juice

Total Servings: 1
Serving Size: 8 ounces

This juice gives my stiff joints a kick! The natural spiciness from the ginger just kicks up this traditional recipe like never before. Carrot juice alone is good, but carrot ginger juice is on a whole different level! So, if you are missing some spice in your life give this drink a try!

4 large carrots, tops removed

½-inch ginger root

¼ cup water

½ cup ice (optional)

1 Process the carrots and ginger in a juice extractor (juicer). Insert the carrots into the juicer first followed by the ginger root. Be sure to follow the manufacturer's instructions as indicated with your machine.

2 Add carrot juice and water to a large glass and stir; if desired, serve over ice.

Tidbits

Ginger has excellent anti-inflammatory properties and a strong, spicy taste so a small piece used will be noticeable. If you do not like ginger, just omit.

If you do not like carrot juice, simply substitute carrots with oranges or apples. If using oranges, peel oranges before processing in the juicer.

NUTRITION FACTS

Based on a 2000 calorie diet per day

	Recipe Nutrition Per Serving	Daily Recommended Nutrition
Calories (kcal)	141	2000
Fat (g)	.01	65
Saturated Fat (g)	0	20
Trans Fat (g)	0	
Poly Unsat Fat (g)	0	
Mono Unsat Fat (g)	0	
Cholesterol (mg)	0	300
Sodium (mg)	160	2400
Carbohydrates (g)	32	300
Dietary Fiber (g)	8	25
Total Sugars (g)	20	
Protein (g)	4	50
Vitamin A (IU)	54,000	5000
Vitamin C (mg)	24	60
Calcium (mg)	80	1000
Iron (mg)	.01	18

Recipe Nutrition Per Serving

Daily Recommended Nutrition

Mint Ginger Tea

Total Servings: 4
Serving Size: 1 cup

I stood in front of an opened fridge, longing for an icy cold beverage—something sweet and delicious without all the unnecessary sugars. Nothing in the fridge resembled that, all I had were herbs and spices; so I decided to get creative and made a chilled sweet mint ginger tea. Whether served hot or cold, this tea is refreshing and very simple to prepare.

4 cups water

1 cup fresh mint leaves, rinsed

5 (⅛-inch thick) slices fresh ginger

3 tablespoons agave nectar syrup

1. Put the water, mint, ginger and agave syrup into a 1½-quart saucepan and bring to a boil. Remove the saucepan from the heat and let tea infuse (or steep) for 1 hour, or until desired taste. The longer the tea steeps, the more intense the flavor will be.)
2. Strain tea into a large pitcher using a large mesh strainer. If desired, refrigerate tea prior to serving.

Tidbit

This recipe can be used with other varieties of herbs and spices such as tarragon, lemongrass, cinnamon, etc. If using tea bags, use 8 ounces water for every bag and steep tea for about 30 minutes before removing the bags.

NUTRITION FACTS

Based on a 2000 calorie diet per day

	Recipe Nutrition Per Serving	Daily Recommended Nutrition
Calories (kcal)	85	2000
Fat (g)	0.5	65
Saturated Fat (g)	0.1	20
Trans Fat (g)	0	
Poly Unsat Fat (g)	0.3	
Mono Unsat Fat (g)	.02	
Cholesterol (mg)	0	300
Sodium (mg)	18	2400
Carbohydrates (g)	21	300
Dietary Fiber (g)	5	25
Total Sugars (g)	11	
Protein (g)	2	50
Vitamin A (IU)	2408	5000
Vitamin C (mg)	18	60
Calcium (mg)	138	1000
Iron (mg)	3	18

Recipe Nutrition Per Serving

Daily Recommended Nutrition

Old Fashioned Lemonade

Total Servings: 6
Serving Size: 1 cup

This refreshing drink is an old time classic that needs no big introduction. Lemonade has always been a staple beverage in my house as a child. I remember those days of rolling lots of lemons trying to soften them before squeezing all of the juice into a bowl. I have upgraded from the days of rolling lemons, but I haven't replaced the love I have for this all-time classic, refreshing drink!

2½ large lemons, peeled and seeded (or ½ cup fresh lemon juice)

6¼ cups water

¾ cup plus 2 teaspoons agave nectar syrup

1 Process the peeled lemons in a juice extractor (juicer). Be sure to follow the manufacturer's instructions as indicated with your machine.

2 Add lemon juice, water and syrup to a large pitcher and stir. Serve chilled.

Tidbits

If you do not have a juicer, roll the lemons until they become soft. Halve lemons and squeeze until all juice has been extracted. (Additional lemons may be needed to obtain ½ cup juice.) Filter juice using a mesh strainer to remove seeds and pulp.

To make green tea lemonade, before adding the water to the juice, bring 4 cups of the water to a brisk boil. Pour the water over 6 tea bags in a large pitcher; let steep for 10 to 15 minutes. Remove the tea bags and mix tea with the lemon juice, syrup and the remaining 2½ cups water with a large spoon. Add additional syrup if needed.

NUTRITION FACTS

Based on a 2000 calorie diet per day

Nutrient	Recipe Nutrition Per Serving	Daily Recommended Nutrition
Calories (kcal)	132	2000
Fat (g)	0	65
Saturated Fat (g)	0	20
Trans Fat (g)	0	
Poly Unsat Fat (g)	0	
Mono Unsat Fat (g)	0	
Cholesterol (mg)	0	300
Sodium (mg)	0.2	2400
Carbohydrates (g)	36	300
Dietary Fiber (g)	2	25
Total Sugars (g)	32	
Protein (g)	0.1	50
Vitamin A (IU)	4	5000
Vitamin C (mg)	1	60
Calcium (mg)	9	1000
Iron (mg)	.01	18

Recipe Nutrition Per Serving

Daily Recommended Nutrition

Hazelnut Latte

Total Servings: 1
Serving Size: 8 ounces

I love the coffee experience—from the sound to the aromatic smells to the taste, all are important when making the perfect shot with my espresso machine. The hazelnut milk compliments the nutty flavor of the brewed espresso and makes this latte the best I've ever tasted!

1½ tablespoons ground espresso

¾ cup hazelnut milk (or rice milk)

4 drops liquid vanilla stevia (or ⅛ teaspoon stevia powder)

1 dash ground nutmeg (optional garnish)

1 Follow the manufacturer's instructions as indicated with your machine, but in general there are a few basic steps for brewing espresso that are common regardless of the equipment. To start, fill the water receptacle with water (make sure the machine is off). Pour enough water to brew the espresso and steam the milk; do not overfill.

2 Fill a steaming pitcher with the milk and place a thermometer securely inside the pitcher. Insert the steaming wand into the milk and turn on the steaming wand switch; the wand should be at an angle (diagonal and not straight). Hold the pitcher at a diagonal and move it around, slowly, to create the froth; continue until the thermometer reaches 100°F. Lower the wand into the milk and heat milk completely, until the thermometer reaches between 160°F to 165°F (anything above that could scorch the milk). Turn off the steaming wand switch and set milk aside until ready for use.

3 Fill the portafilter (or brewing cup) with ground espresso and tamper firmly to pack down the espresso. Place a receptacle (like a one-ounce shot glass) underneath the portafilter, and turn the machine on. The espresso brew should start trickling into the receptacle.

4 Pour the brewed espresso into a heatproof cup, and stir in the stevia. Pour the steamed milk over the espresso. When pouring use a spoon to regulate the flow of the foam. Make sure no foam enters the drink until about ¼-inch from the top of the cup. If desired, garnish the top with ground nutmeg.

Tidbit

If you do not have an espresso machine, just prepare the espresso using a coffee maker. Follow the instructions indicated with your coffee equipment.

NUTRITION FACTS

Based on a 2000 calorie diet per day

	Recipe Nutrition Per Serving	Daily Recommended Nutrition
Calories (kcal)	97	2000
Fat (g)	3	65
Saturated Fat (g)	.03	20
Trans Fat (g)	0	
Poly Unsat Fat (g)	.03	
Mono Unsat Fat (g)	0	
Cholesterol (mg)	0	300
Sodium (mg)	94	2400
Carbohydrates (g)	17	300
Dietary Fiber (g)	1	25
Total Sugars (g)	11	
Protein (g)	2	50
Vitamin A (IU)	375	5000
Vitamin C (mg)	.06	60
Calcium (mg)	226	1000
Iron (mg)	0.3	18

Cinnamon Apple Cider

Total Servings: 1½
Serving Size: 1 cup

When I worked at a coffee shop, I learned how to make apple cider drinks during the winter months. I was surprised to see that the base of the drink was just apple juice purchased at the local grocery store! So, I decided to start making my own simple version at home.

4 medium apples (about 3-inch round)

½ cup water

¼ teaspoon ground cinnamon

⅛ teaspoon ground cloves

½ teaspoon honey (optional)

1 cinnamon stick (optional)

1. Process apples in a juice extractor (juicer). Be sure to follow the manufacturer's instructions as indicated with your machine.
2. Whisk juice, cinnamon and cloves in a small saucepan, and simmer, covered, over low heat, stirring continually, about 3 to 5 minutes, or until hot. If desired, add honey, if cider is not sweet. Serve in a large mug and garnish with a pinch of cinnamon and cinnamon stick.

Tidbits

After the cider settles, the juice will start to separate from the pulp. However, if you do not like the pulp, filter using a fine mesh. If you do not have a juicer, use 1 cup unfiltered, organic apple juice and follow as instructed above.

NUTRITION FACTS

Based on a 2000 calorie diet per day

	Recipe Nutrition Per Serving	Daily Recommended Nutrition
Calories (kcal)	253	2000
Fat (g)	1	65
Saturated Fat (g)	0.1	20
Trans Fat (g)	0	
Poly Unsat Fat (g)	0.3	
Mono Unsat Fat (g)	.04	
Cholesterol (mg)	0	300
Sodium (mg)	5	2400
Carbohydrates (g)	67	300
Dietary Fiber (g)	12	25
Total Sugars (g)	50	
Protein (g)	1	50
Vitamin A (IU)	263	5000
Vitamin C (mg)	22	60
Calcium (mg)	33	1000
Iron (mg)	1	18

Recipe Nutrition Per Serving

Daily Recommended Nutrition

Peppermint Hot Chocolate

Total Servings: 1
Serving Size: 1 cup

I have many fond memories of using the little pre-packaged, pre-sweetened hot chocolate mixes. Now that I have moved to an artificial ingredients-free lifestyle, I prepare my hot chocolate the old fashioned way—using unsweetened cocoa powder, milk, and sweetener. Prior to working at a coffee shop, my hot chocolate was basic. But after a few weeks of trying new things, I fell in love with peppermint hot chocolate!

1 cup hazelnut milk (or any non-dairy milk)

Dash of peppermint extract (about ½ cap size)

1 tablespoon unsweetened cocoa powder

⅛ teaspoon stevia powder (or 2 droplets liquid stevia)

Heat all ingredients over medium heat in a small saucepan; stir continually with a whisk until all ingredients have dissolved. You will see tiny bubbles around the sides of the pot. Pour hot chocolate milk into a thermal insulated cup.

Tidbits

Try this same recipe with carob powder. Carob is naturally sweet so there is no need to add the stevia powder. Chocolate naturally has caffeine, so peppermint hot carob is a great substitute if you don't want the caffeine.

The milk can also be heated in the microwave or by using an espresso machine. Follow the instructions indicated with your equipment.

NUTRITION FACTS

Based on a 2000 calorie diet per day

	Recipe Nutrition Per Serving	Daily Recommended Nutrition
Calories (kcal)	130	2000
Fat (g)	4	65
Saturated Fat (g)	0	20
Trans Fat (g)	0	
Poly Unsat Fat (g)	0	
Mono Unsat Fat (g)	0	
Cholesterol (mg)	0	300
Sodium (mg)	120	2400
Carbohydrates (g)	21	300
Dietary Fiber (g)	4	25
Total Sugars (g)	14	
Protein (g)	2	50
Vitamin A (IU)	500	5000
Vitamin C (mg)	0	60
Calcium (mg)	300	1000
Iron (mg)	1	18

Recipe Nutrition Per Serving

Daily Recommended Nutrition

Glossary

This glossary includes a brief definition or description of key food and health vocabularies that were used throughout this cookbook.

Agave nectar syrup – Agave nectar syrup is a sweetener that comes from the blue agave cactus plant.

Buckwheat – Buckwheat, despite the common name and the grain-like use of the crop, is a fruit seed that is related to rhubarb; consequently, it is not a grass and is not related to wheat.

Carob – Carob powder is made from the ground seeds and pods of the carob tree. Carob is naturally sweet and is used as a chocolate substitute.

Celtic Sea Salt® Brand – Celtic Sea Salt® Brand is authentic, unprocessed sea salt that is free of pesticides, anti-caking or bleaching agents and is hand-harvested in France.

Currants – Currants (also known as Zante) are made from dried grapes that are one-fourth the size of raisins.

Gumbo Filé – Gumbo Filé, also called filé powder, is a spice made from dried and ground sassafras leaves. It is used sparingly in gumbo as thickening agent, giving it a distinctive flavor and texture.

Flaxseeds – Flaxseeds contain high levels Omega-3 fatty acids, which may benefit the heart. Flaxseeds have a slight nutty flavor and range from deep amber to reddish brown color depending upon whether the flax is of the golden or brown variety.

Food allergy – Food allergies occur when the immune system rejects food, causing reactions such as throat swelling, cramps or severe and life-threatening conditions. These immune system reactions can occur immediately when the food is ingested or at a later time (about 1 to 3 days) after the food has been ingested.

Food intolerance – Food intolerance is the inability to properly digest or process certain foods. Food intolerances do not impact the immune system but usually triggers a digestive reaction.

Gluten – Gluten is the mixture of proteins found in wheat grains such as rye, wheat and barley. Gluten gives wheat dough its elastic texture.

Guar gum – Guar gum, a natural gum, is an edible thickening agent extracted from the guar bean.

Leeks – Leeks are related to onions, shallots and scallions (green onions). They look like large scallions having a very small bulb and a long white cylindrical stalk of superimposed layers that wraps into green, tightly wrapped, flat leaves.

Millet flour – Millet is a grain that has been in existence for many centuries and is widely produced around the world—India and Africa are the top producers. Millet does not contain gluten, but has a similar protein profile as wheat.

Quinoa – Quinoa is a 6000 year old seed that originated out of the Andes Mountain of South America. Quinoa is not a grain though it is cooked and eaten as a grain. It has the most protein than any other grain and it is a complete protein containing all nine essential amino acids that the body needs.

Stevia – Stevia is made from the plant rebaudiana and claims to have up to 300 times the sweetness of sugar. It has no calories and no glycemic index; it is all natural and does not contain acetic acid, formaldehyde, chloride, etc.

Tahini – Tahini is ground, lightly roasted sesame seeds; it is very typical in Middle Eastern cuisine.

Stay connected with Rhonda by visiting the website: www.rhondascooking.com. You can also follow Rhonda on www.twitter.com/rhondascooking and www.facebook.com/rhondascooking.

If you have any questions concerning these recipes or any products used in these recipes, email info@rhondascooking.com or write to the following address:

5130 W. Baseline Road, Suite 117, PMB 118
Laveen, AZ 85339

www.rhondascooking.com

Index